MW00339751

HIDDEN HISTORY
of
OLD LYME, LYME
& EAST LYME

HIDDEN HISTORY
of
OLD LYME, LYME & EAST LYME

Jim Lampos and Michaelle Pearson

THE
History
PRESS

Published by The History Press
Charleston, SC
www.historypress.com

Copyright © 2020 by Jim Lampos and Michaelle Pearson
All rights reserved

Cover: Ye Golden Spur Inn, Ye Golden Spur Park, on the New London and East Lyme Street Railway. *Elizabeth Kuchta collection.*

First published 2020

Manufactured in the United States

ISBN 9781467143400

Library of Congress Control Number: 2020930487

Notice: The information in this book is true and complete to the best of our knowledge. It is offered without guarantee on the part of the authors or The History Press. The authors and The History Press disclaim all liability in connection with the use of this book.

All rights reserved. No part of this book may be reproduced or transmitted in any form whatsoever without prior written permission from the publisher except in the case of brief quotations embodied in critical articles and reviews.

To our children, Phoebe and Silvanos, with love.

CONTENTS

PREFACE

You don't have to listen very hard—the land itself prompts questions: why's that there? What's this all about? We see things in our daily commute that remain with us as lingering curiosities, which in the rush and thrum of making a buck and living our lives, we often don't have time to explore. I guess that's why we write history books—it's an excuse to investigate. It's permission to stop time, borrow a minute to sneak off the highway and check out that old dam, that pile of stones, that weird crook in the road or that impossibly old tree. The funny thing is, they all have stories to tell. And their stories are ours. The land made decisions for us long ago—how we made our living, how we made our way to-and-fro. And we, in turn, made our mark on the land. The choices of our illustrious predecessors, to a great extent, still guide our steps today. We are under the sway of their thoughts; we travel their routes; we repurpose their constructions. As the land made them and they made their mark on the landscape, so, too, do we engage with them—and in this dance of the past and present, we create the future. This book is dedicated to the hope of an enlightened journey in the days to come.

A NOTE ON PLACE NAMES AND LANGUAGE

For those unfamiliar with the area, all this talk about the "Lymes" may be a bit confusing. Today's Old Lyme, East Lyme and Lyme were once one town called Lyme, a political entity that corresponded to the Lyme parish of the Congregational church. As the population grew in the eighteenth century, a second parish, or "society," was established in the eastern portion of town, with another in the north part of town. In the nineteenth century, these three societies each became their own towns. The second society became the town of East Lyme in 1839, and the first society and north society became the towns of Old Lyme and Lyme, respectively. Today, while the three towns have a shared identity, each also retains its own unique character. Lyme is the most rural, maintaining its agrarian tradition. Old Lyme remains a traditional New England hamlet, while East Lyme has embraced modern development.

Adding to the confusion are the villages within each town, some of which have a more defined character than the town itself. Niantic, in East Lyme, is a good example. Today, it is known as a seaside community of charming cottages and shops, though its identity as a distinct entity goes back to Algonquin times, as it was the center of the Nehantic tribe. Flanders, also in East Lyme, has an entirely different character. In the nineteenth century, it was home to a thriving group of mills, and it remains a commercial district today, though the mills have been replaced by strip malls. Similarly, some neighborhoods in Old Lyme and Lyme maintain their own special character, such as Lyme's Hamburg section or Silltown in Old Lyme. Confusing though these distinctions may be, they are part and parcel of the quirkiness that makes the Lymes so alluring.

As we discuss the various parts of these towns, we may use place names anachronistically; we may, for example, refer to Old Lyme in 1750, when in fact no such town existed. It was simply called Lyme. This was done for the sake of clarity, so the reader may understand where a place would be located in the modern landscape.

Similarly, the reader will notice some nonstandard spellings or word usage in quotes from early town records, letters and memorials. We have chosen to retain the idiosyncratic spelling of these original documents to convey the flavor of the language at the time.

ACKNOWLEDGEMENTS

The authors wish to thank the following organizations for their kind assistance:

Connecticut Historical Society
Connecticut River Museum
Connecticut Spiritualist Camp Meeting Association
Connecticut State Library
East Lyme Historical Society
East Lyme Library
East Lyme Town Hall
Indian and Colonial Research Center
Lyme Grange No. 147
Lyme Public Hall and Local History Archives
Lyme Public Library
Lyme Town Hall
New York Public Library
Old Lyme Historical Society
Old Lyme Phoebe Griffin Noyes Library
University of Connecticut Library, Thomas J. Dodd Research Center Archives and Special Collections

With special thanks to Linda Alexander, Arthur "Skip" Beebe, Nancy Beebe, Carolyn Bacdayan, Tara Borden, George Carfi, Maureen Caswell,

Acknowledgements

Sandra Downing, Baylee Drown, Katie Huffman, Ellis Jewett, Elizabeth Kuchta, Mark Lander, Eric Lehman, Marcus Mason Maronn, Dani McGrath, James Meehan, Alison Mitchell, Amy Nawrocki, Mary Jo Nosal, John Pfeiffer, John Pote, Cathy Shields, Laura Smith and Abigail Stokes.

I

THE BURYING GROUND

The dead tell no tales, it is said, and perhaps that's true. But their gravestones do, and on a morning when the fog hangs low, swirling like a wraith among the sandstones, granites and slates, a curious explorer in the Duck River Cemetery, along the banks of the river that lends its name, will be rewarded with true tales and fanciful myths told from the earliest mists of Lyme's history. These are the stories we have told ourselves for three centuries and more and that mold who we are as citizens of this seacoast town.

On Memorial Day, all and sundry march down Lyme Street, following flags, fire trucks, fife and drums corps and schoolchildren into the cemetery, where they will honor dead and living veterans and hear fine speeches from venerable neighbors and luminaries. The ceremony will end with a three-round salute, fired amid gravestones dating to the seventeenth century, and thus the living will commune with the dead and honor them, as the departed live among us still—the legacy of their deeds forming and informing our world.

It seems fitting and proper that the founding myth of a New England town of considerable antiquity should concern a vow to preserve and protect the grave and memory of a beautiful, red-haired lady and, in exchange, a considerable estate would be granted. Such is the case with the founding of Lyme. Matthew Griswold was given his estate, Black Hall, at the mouth of the Connecticut River in exchange for a promise to perpetually care for the grave of Lady Fenwick. This legend has more than a grain of truth to it, as Griswold is known as one of Connecticut's early gravestone carvers, who not only fashioned Lady Fenwick's table stone in Saybrook but also carved those of the colony's earliest founders, which can still be found at the Ancient Burying Ground in Hartford. Now in their twelfth generation, the direct descendants of the first Matthew Griswold still reside at Black Hall and maintain Lady Fenwick's grave and keep her memory, as promised.

Much can be learned from a town's burying ground. Quickly glancing at some of Lyme's earliest resting places, one notices the oldest gravestones, made of sandstone and slate, near the entrance. In a town known for its granite, this seems unusual. But Lyme was a seafaring town, and these stones did not come from the quarries of its countryside, but instead were carved and shipped from Boston, Newport or the famous brownstone quarries of Portland, thirty miles up the Connecticut River. These soft but durable stones allowed the carvers, working by hand, to create subtle and intricate designs and led to the rise of the earliest expression of New England folk art in the Connecticut River Valley, in a practical form memorializing the dead and creating a written and visual record of those who had come before.

Some of the oldest stones, such as that of Reynold Marvin at Old Lyme's Duck River Cemetery, were carved by James Stanclift (1634–1712). In 1684, Stanclift arrived in Connecticut from the island of Nevis and settled in Lyme. The next year, he married "the Widow Waller," also known as Mary Tinker Waller, wife of the late William Waller. The Widow Waller turns up frequently in the Lyme records as a landholder of some significance, and she is one of two women listed as "proprietors" of Lyme in 1677, which means that she had full voting rights at town meetings. Stanclift married well. In February 1686, he was given permission by the Town of Lyme to make bricks on the banks of the Connecticut River near Lords Lane. Stanclift's reputation as a mason and stonecarver quickly grew, and in 1690, the Town of Middletown made him an offer he couldn't refuse.

Middletown offered Stanclift a land grant on the east side of the Connecticut River, which had a rich deposit of the sedimentary rock that came to be known as brownstone, in exchange for his skills as a carver and stoneworker. Today's town of Portland was then part of Middletown, and the land grant that Stanclift was offered came to be known as the Portland Brownstone Quarry. He was the first owner of the quarry, which operated from 1690 until 2012, when it finally closed for good. It is now a state park and recreation area, but its vast deposit of brownstone is still evident, as is its impact on the architecture of the United States.

James Stanclift I: Grave of Joseph Sill, 1696, Duck River Cemetery. *Jim Lampos.*

Found everywhere from Canada to San Francisco, it is estimated that 80 percent of the brownstone used in New York City during the nineteenth century came from the Portland quarry. It provided the material with which the elegant mansions of the Vanderbilts, Astors and Rothschilds were built and the charming rowhouses of Manhattan and Brooklyn were faced. Locally, New London's public library and Broad Street courthouse are made of brownstone, as is much of the original campus of Wesleyan University. In the oldest burying grounds of our region, we find that the earliest gravestones are carved from this same material.

James Stanclift's stones are easily recognized and can still be easily found in Connecticut, Massachusetts and Long Island. Low to the ground with semicircular tops, the stones are carved in all capital letters, providing the basic facts of the person interred beneath. Name, date of birth and date of death is all one will find, with no embellishments or artistic devices. Even this spare memorial was elaborate for the earliest citizens of Lyme—prior to Stanclift, most graves were marked with a single rock or a pile of gathered fieldstones in the manner of the native Nehantics or not marked at all. One notices that the area near the entrance of these oldest burying grounds often

William Stanclift: Grave of John Lay, 1723, Meeting House Hill Cemetery. *Jim Lampos.*

appears empty or devoid of monuments, while in fact, this is often where the earliest graves are to be found. With Stanclift, one finds, for the first time, a celebration or at least a commemoration of individuals in the community. And that this celebration, carved in stone, has survived so remarkably well for more than three hundred years, through New England's notoriously inclement weather and thoughtlessly drunken vandals, is a testament to that gentleman's enduring craft.

The next generation of Stanclift gravestone carvers, sons William (1687–1761) and James II (1692–1772), added some artistic embellishments that would have been frowned on in their father's era. The stones carved by James II feature artistic devices such as a rosette in the elaborated three-part top of the stone, as seen on the memorial of Lieutenant Abraham Brounson, dated 1719. William added his own idiosyncratic touches, like the rather comical death's head on the stone of John Lay, carved in 1723. They were but trying to keep up with the times, as such embellishments were craved by the leading lights of Newport and Boston, and desire is contagious.

Beginning in the 1720s, Thomas Johnson (1690–1761) partnered with the Stanclifts in the brownstone quarry and began what would be his family's

Thomas Johnson II (Deacon): Grave of Timothy Mather, 1755, Duck River Cemetery. *Jim Lampos.*

tradition of gravestone carving using Portland brownstone. Each successive generation of his heirs reflected the changing social attitudes of Lyme. The work of Thomas I features grim skulls with empty eye sockets, hollow nasal cavities and gritting teeth, reminding the living of the certainty of death and the final fate of the body. In the 1730s, one begins to see recognizably human features in the work of Thomas Johnson II (Deacon Johnson), and by the 1740s, fashionable gravestones had "soul effigies" that more closely resembled living human faces, with wings representing the soul in flight and sometimes crowned to represent the glory of the afterlife. The borders of the stones are elaborately decorated with vines, flowers and other pleasing devices. So, too, the epitaphs begin to give some of the particulars of the individual, including their station in life or accomplishments, attesting that their loss is grieved by the living. These stones express sentiments affirming the hope that, in illuminating the life of the departed, the soul will be justly rewarded in the afterlife.

What accounts for this shift? The first English settlers in Lyme, antimonarchist in politics, puritan in religion and bound to each other for material survival, valued community over the individual. Their cause was a common one, with no time for sentimental mourning. Thus, their early graves were marked by the simple stones at hand. By the 1730s and 1740s, the region's economy was growing, and the town of Lyme was, by all accounts, strong and successful. The Great Awakening, a religious evangelical movement, swept through, with its emphasis on the individual experience of salvation over deeds and ecstatic expression of faith over dour and staid ritual. More than this, the colonial families were now in their third and fourth generations, and while the early pioneers were well aware of their inevitable death and the possibility that they could disappear off the earth without trace or remembrance and had to trust in God for their eternal salvation, the well-established and comfortable Lyme families of 1740 could think about their ancestors, look forward to their progeny and muse about posterity. Thus the gravestones of their dead grew larger, more personal, and more elaborate, just as their homes had gone from simple capes and gambrels to stately colonial mansions. They looked forward to the future with artistic touches and human faces attached to the soul, with winged hope for eternal salvation and an afterlife that carried with it the honor of the earthly life. It was not just the fact of the grave—the finality of life to which they were resigned as their ancestors had been—it was the promise of immortality in both a spiritual and material sense, as their names might forever be on the lips of their descendants through the ages.

The symbolic figures on the gravestones became less allegorical and more realistic as the century progressed. Unrelated to the Thomas Johnson family, a Durham-based carver by the name of John Johnson (1748–1826) became famous for his particularly expressive faces with big noses and eyes looking heavenward with a mix of expectation and dread. Some of his soul effigies seem positively crestfallen with a look of "Oh, Lord, why me?" John Isham's stones, on other hand, are recognized by the narrow noses of his elegant, but serenely expressionless, soul effigies.

The Lymes' burying grounds feature the works of other notable carvers whose distinct hands are evident in their work. Ebenezer Drake used a lovely brick-red sandstone from the quarries near his Windsor home, and his distinctive cherubs have individualized, lifelike features that make one wonder if they were modeled on the deceased. An unknown artisan dubbed the "Glastonbury Lady Carver" by gravestone scholar Ernest Caulfield is so named because his work is found chiefly in the Glastonbury area and often features feminine figures, albeit some rather ludicrously rendered ones. The stone he fashioned for John Alger in the Duck River Cemetery features a skull that looks like a jack-o'-lantern with wild, witchy hair. Another carver with a rather cartoonish hand was the "hook and eye man," Gershom Bartlett, whose schist stones from the quarries of Bolton are immediately recognizable by their balloon-headed soul effigies.

Stones by a group of carvers collectively known as "the Boston School" are commonly found as well. Boston was an artistic and political hub in the eighteenth century, and its stoneworkers were known as the most adept. While much scholarship still remains to be done to identify the individuals responsible for each stone, some can be attributed with confidence. The beautifully preserved slate in the Wait Cemetery is certainly the work of

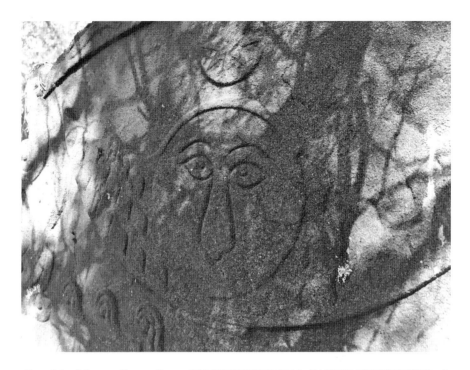

Above: John Johnson: Grave of Phebe Beckwith, 1791, Wait Cemetery. *Jim Lampos.*

Right: Ebenezer Drake: Grave of Enoch Sill, 1777, Duck River Cemetery. *Jim Lampos.*

Boston-area carver John Just Geyer. Many of the tombstones from the Boston area were quarried in the vicinity of Apthorp Street in the Norfolk Downs section of Quincy, near the bay. Slate Island, just off the coast of nearby Hingham was another source of the easily carved but durable stone, with quarrying operations there beginning as early as 1631.

The Narragansett basin in Rhode Island was yet another center of stone carving, with its lovely and durable slates. The meticulously carved massive blue slates made by George Allen and his son Gabriel attract the eye immediately upon entering Lyme's burial grounds and remain in a remarkable state of preservation. But perhaps the most elegant artistry of this era is evidenced in the work of the Stevens Shop of Newport, the oldest continuously operating business in America. Its distinctive green and deep blue slate stones can be found here and there in Lyme graveyards, including Plant's Dam in Old Lyme and Old Stone Church in East Lyme. Its bald cherubs with pursed lips and articulated borders with delicate filigrees appear almost Art Nouveau in their design.

The attractive gravestones of the Stevens family shop speak to a tasteful aesthetic that the prosperous living can afford to bestow upon their dead. Founder John Stevens opened the shop in 1705. His descendants ran the shop until 1927, when it was sold to native Newporter John Howard Benson. It has remained in Benson's family since. His son, John Everett Benson, carved John F. Kennedy's tombstone at Arlington National Cemetery, and his grandson Nicholas Benson carved the Martin Luther King Memorial in Washington. The Bensons have become known as among the best current stone carvers in the world, and they have continued this great operative and artistic tradition of stonework today. In Old Lyme, a modern stone marker on Ferry Road memorializing Revolutionary War general Samuel Holden Parsons was carved by the Stevens Shop circa 1980.

Stevens Shop stones found locally date primarily from the 1760s, a period that saw fervent communication and commerce between Lyme and Newport. The Congregational ministers of each town, the revolutionary firebrand Stephen Johnson and leading intellectual divine Ezra Stiles, were the best of friends and often visited each other. Like the realm of ideas, friendship and commerce, the traffic in stones was not one way. Lyme, too, sent its quarried rock to Newport. The distinctive granite known as "Black Hall granite" or "Lyme Pink" was exported in the nineteenth century and used to build Newport's lovely Channing Memorial Church. Around Lyme, one need only look at Center School on Lyme Street to see an example of our local granite as a building façade. And while today the granite quarries have

The Stevens Shop (John II or William): Grave of Daniel Sterlin, 1760, Old Stone Church Burial Ground. *Jim Lampos.*

generally fallen silent and reverted back to their natural state, there are still active gravel pits in the Lymes, and every night a Providence and Worcester freight train rumbles down the shoreline through East Lyme and Old Lyme, continuing west down the coast and, upon entering New York City, crosses the Hell Gate Bridge on its way to the Atlantic freight yard in Maspeth, Queens, where it will unload its Connecticut gravel—about a million tons a year—to feed the endlessly hungry maw of Gotham's construction industry.

Luminescent in the morning sun, among the most evocative stones in the Duck River Cemetery are the simple granite markers done by an itinerant artisan named Peter Barker, who traveled from town to town carving stones using the materials at hand—in our case, Black Hall granite. Though the inscriptions are difficult to read due to their shallow strike in the pegmatite's hard surface, they are still legible to the patient and dedicated, and the overall effect in the foggy dew of dawn is one of elevating reverence for both the spirits of the dead and of the land. Perhaps even more beautiful are the granites of John Hartshorne, with their distinctive borders of inverted hearts, Celtic crosses, snakes, mazes

John Hartshorne: Grave of William Minor, 1725, Old Stone Church Burial Ground. *Jim Lampos.*

and moon-like faces. Hartshorne was a man of seventy years when he arrived in this region from Boston, but his striking memorials, each one unique, exhibit the vigor of an artist in his prime.

Lyme's sturdy granite endures as the inexhaustible bones of our land. The outcrops on hilltops reach down to the bowels of the earth, formed millions of years ago in a forge of fire, worn and scraped by wind and ice over millennia. When the first people roamed this corner of the earth a little over ten thousand years ago, stone was a fact of the land. It pointed the way, delineated boundaries and provided material for tools—arrowheads, hammers, mortars and pestles. The Algonquin tribes who supplanted the first people used glacial erratics to create sacred space to memorialize their dead, with venerated souls buried on a knoll overlooking a stream facing west. A walk in the woods for those who recognize their signs is rewarded with lovely vistas and deeply meditative episodes of beauty in a landscape reclaimed by the flora and fauna that had once been stripped by colonization and industrialization. Their work endures, but the years are measured in thousands not hundreds.

It is poetically just, perhaps, that the grave of Lyme's first English settler and stone carver, Matthew Griswold I, remains unmarked and its whereabouts unknown. For his estate, Black Hall, was itself a Native American settlement and burial ground, with graves unmarked or unknown until archaeological digs under the auspices of Yale University in 1939 and 1940 revealed burials, along with fireplaces, hearths and shell heaps. The burials were oriented to the west, as this beautiful knoll at the mouth of the Connecticut River has a splendid view of the sun setting over the Long Island Sound, giving all souls—native and immigrant, living and departed—access to the transcendental beauty of the summer lands.

THE PERSISTENCE OF MEMORY

S ome towns like to flaunt their antiquity, but citizens of the Lymes quietly go about their lives, keeping their architectural treasures hidden in plain sight. A ride down any of the old roads, such as Mile Creek, Johnnycake Hill, Short Hills or Shore Road rewards the traveler with numerous examples of houses from the "first period," the late 1600s and early 1700s. Capes and gambrels abound, some preserved and open to the public and others continuing to fulfill their original function as family homes.

In Old Lyme, we find one of the oldest Cape Cod–style houses in the nation—the circa 1666 Joseph Peck house. Shortly thereafter, gambrels made their appearance with their roof lines resembling a ship's hull. It is said that shipwrights introduced this design, which made the upper floor more useful. A fine example of this style is the 1690 Captain Chadwick house on Mile Creek Road. Both capes and gambrels were built around a center chimney, with stairs winding around to the upper sleeping loft. As families grew and prospered, so did their houses. Capes acquired second floors and became Colonials. Lean-tos were added to Colonials, transforming them into Saltboxes with catslide roofs.

The Thomas Lee house on West Main Street in East Lyme is probably the best local example of the Saltbox style. The oldest part of the house is thought to date to 1660, with later additions over the following century. Now a museum, the beautifully preserved house brings visitors into the atmosphere of the Lymes' earliest days. The 1685 Samuel Smith house on nearby Plant's Dam Road is also open to the public.

Chadwick house circa 1690. *James Meehan.*

Peck house circa 1660. *James Meehan.*

In 1934, the Old Lyme Guild of Artists and Craftsmen moved into the Peck Tavern. Founders Roger Griswold, Elinor Sears, Beatrice Hoffman, Caro Ely and Nathaniel Hall on opening day. *Old Lyme Historical Society Archive.*

The north town green in Old Lyme boasts one of the most elegant and celebrated houses of this period—the Peck Tavern. Built circa 1675 as a family home, by the turn of the eighteenth century, it hosted a tavern, and in the 1750s, it housed John McCurdy's store. During the Revolutionary War, it was said that the tavern provided food and clothing to passing soldiers who often camped on the green outside. The most famous legend attached to the Peck Tavern concerns a curious architectural quirk—a wall dividing the two front rooms on the second floor, which can be swung up and hooked into the ceiling, creating a large ballroom. This wall on the ceiling is complete with a door, which results in a strange and whimsical sight—a testament to the ingenuity of colonial architects. It is said that George Washington danced in this ballroom one evening as he was passing through Lyme. As John McCurdy was his host, and McCurdy's store was on the premises, it is certainly possible that Washington, who was known to have loved a minuet and reel, was entertained here. But since we have yet to find a witness to the event, we can't attest to this as fact.

THE TOWN MEETING

The New England town meeting is perhaps the oldest democratic institution in the world. The citizens of Lyme have been meeting to decide their civic affairs since the town's founding in 1665. Through wars, religious and political upheavals, revolution, plagues and pandemics, they have met to chart the course of their town. To be sure, it was not a perfect democracy in the beginning, and it is not one now, as no democracy can perfectly represent the will of the people. However, by the standards of the seventeenth century, it was remarkably inclusive, and by today's standards, the current form of the town meeting in Lyme, East Lyme and Old Lyme stands out as a uniquely empowering forum through which average citizens can make their voices heard, their opinions noted and their votes counted. All budget matters must be approved at town meeting, just as any decisions concerning laws, ordinances, regulations or major town initiatives must pass muster with the citizenry. There is no intermediary town council, no city manager has the power to dictate policy and no mayor can exercise executive prerogative. The board of selectmen, which oversees the town's affairs, must rule by the consent of the governed. One person, one vote. If a special interest tries to take over a town, it has to do more than cozy up to a handful of elected officials. It has to find favor with each individual voter as well, and that takes more than just throwing a little money and weight around.

In the seventeenth and eighteenth centuries, not every citizen was allowed a vote at the meeting. One had to be a property owner. Thus slaves,

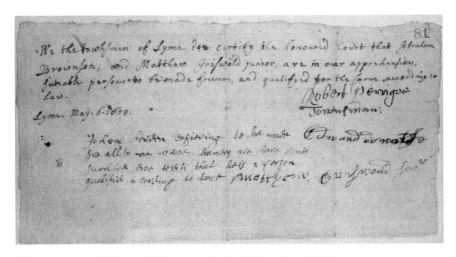

"Freemen accepted," Lyme 1678. *Connecticut State Library, Samuel Wyllys papers.*

indentured servants, tenant farmers and Native Americans were all excluded from the process. Remarkably, however, in the earliest records of the town, we find that some women did vote. In 1675, town meeting minutes show that the Widow Waller was given the measure of land due her late husband. She owned land in her own name and had the right to vote at town meeting. Indeed, she was listed as one of the town's proprietors in the January 14, 1677 town records, along with Widow Marvin.

We shouldn't make too much of this. A woman could not just show up in town, purchase land and become a voting member of the town meeting. The "freemen" of the town, or proprietors, had to be approved by the town meeting at large, just as a co-op board in a modern apartment building must approve new members. Only men could purchase land, and these purchases had to be approved at a meeting and the landowner admitted as a proprietor. But in the early days of the town, women were listed as beneficiaries in their husband's wills, and by virtue of inheritance, were admitted as proprietors at town meeting.

Sometimes the wives were given land at the expense of an adult son. In 1690, John Lay bequeathed his house and land to his wife, Abigail, and made her sole executrix of this will, while his son, James, only received a calf pasture. Perhaps according the family matriarch full citizenship was a matter of necessity in the early days of the town, when unity and consensus among the settlers was key to survival. By the eighteenth century, when the town was prospering, we no longer find women on the town lists.

Town government was intricately entwined with all aspects of society and economy. Indeed, it is impossible to talk about economy and government as separate phenomena in the seventeenth century, as one depended on the other for its very existence. The town either established or regulated nearly all economic activity and was dependent on the prospering of merchants, craftsmen, farmers and all others involved in economic enterprise.

To establish a viable community, the town solicited tradespeople to provide services in exchange for land. In 1672, Leonard Austin was given sixteen acres in exchange for his skills as a weaver. Peter Pratt of Narragansett was given eight acres for his gunsmithing services and, in 1676, was granted additional meadows and upland acreage in exchange for his blacksmithing skills, providing he "tarry four years in the Towne after this date." In 1686, Christopher Christophers was given land in exchange for building a warehouse and agreeing to "supply the town with salt and Barbados goods on reasonable terms." Along with cotton and indigo, "Barbados goods" was synonymous with rum, an essential fuel to stoke that colonial "fire in the belly."

The keeping of taverns and ordinaries was also regulated by the town as early as 1670, when we find John Lay appointed as keeper of the ordinary. In 1674, Balthazar DeWolfe served that role, and in 1702, the duty fell to Joseph Peck. At the same meeting that Peck was made tavern keeper, it was voted that "Thomas Anderson shall have liberty to sell about one hundred gallons of Rum out of jars by the gallon or quart." It looks like Mr. Christopher's warehouse for Barbados goods was humming along nicely.

When government concerns itself with alcohol, it's certain that firearms can't be far behind. The supply of powder and shot was regulated by the town. At the March 31, 1690 town meeting, it was voted that Captain Sill and Joseph Peck "are appointed to supply the inhabitants of Lyme…with powder and lead not half a pound of powder and three pound of lead to each man."

At the July 14 meeting that year, Sill, Peck and Lieutenant Brounson were given "full power to make division and appoint where the town stock of powder and lead shall be disposed of and left with such persons as may be most for the good and safety of this town and the inhabitants thereof." While the town did not concern itself with inhabitants' fowling pieces, rifles and pistols, powder and shot were communally purchased and distributed, and a common store was kept secure under lock and key at the powder house. Even the Nehantics were accorded their allotment—1673 meeting records note that "Mr. Measure shall have liberty to sell powder and lead to the friendly Indians."

In addition to smiths and weavers, coopers and tailors were recruited by the town. At the January 5, 1690 meeting, Arthur Shofel was given money to purchase land, and in return, "Shofel doeht promise and engage to conintue in the town and do the taylors works of the town" for four more years.

In 1698, Nathaniel Hudson was given ten acres, "provided he doth inhabit there upon four years after he doth improve the same and do for the town at the trade of a cooper upon reasonable terms."

Along with laying the foundation on which a solid economy could be built, the town concerned itself with the well-being of its citizens from the very beginning. Relief for the poor and distressed fell on the town, and the earliest records show the town helping the indigent. Among those on the town relief rolls in 1699 was the Jeremiah Moss family. While the town took on the responsibility of providing a safety net for those who met with misfortune, it also took precautions to ensure that newcomers did not fall on the town's welfare rolls. In the August 16, 1705 town meeting minutes, there is a complaint against Thomas Lord Sr. "for the entertaining of widow Hannah Boothe late of Long Island." Lest one think that this complaint was a matter of puritan prudery, the minutes go on to note the real concern, as Lord was ordered to secure "the sum of one hundred pound in current paye of this convenant to be paid to the Town upon any damage the said Town shall sustain by said widow either for her maintenance in sickness or in health." In other words: Tom, we don't care what you get up to with Hannah Boothe, but we sure as blazes are not going to pay her a dime of welfare when you're out of the picture.

From the outset, the town handled the building of roads and bridges, hiring William Waller in 1667 to supervise forty men in bridging the Black Hall and Duck Rivers. Most of the town's primary roads and attendant creek and river crossings date from the late seventeenth to the early eighteenth century, and a map of the Lymes from 1715 would be recognizable today, with only Interstate 95 added as an additional primary route.

The town also handled the conservation of natural resources. As the native forests were clear cut for fuel, building and commerce, wood became a precious commodity. In 1708, the transport of timber from the town's common land was banned by a town meeting vote, and the export of any timber from the town's boundaries was subject to the town's express written permission.

The control of wildlife also fell within the town's purview. In 1720, the town paid two shillings per head for every fox and wildcat, six shillings for every five crows and one penny per woodpecker. Wolves were a particular menace

Old Lyme town meeting, 2019. *James Meehan.*

for local farmers, as sheep livestock were well suited to Lyme's rolling hills and stony land. Members of the Nehantic tribe, who were particularly adept at trapping, were paid twenty shillings per wolf head. White inhabitants of the town were paid forty shillings per head.

The structure of town government reveals the functions it deemed critical. At the head of government stood the three elected townsmen, or selectmen, functioning much as the selectpeople of the town do today. In 1685, the board of selectmen was composed of Thomas Lee, Abram Brounson and Matthew Griswold. Other officials included a town constable, three highway surveyors, two haywards, two fence viewers and two-pound keepers, along with the leather sealer, the brander of horses, the schoolmaster and the eternal bane of citizens since the time of Methuselah, ye olde tax collector.

The striking aspect of Lyme's town government in the late 1600s is how recognizable and similar it is to today. Indeed, much of what we consider to be "modern" American ideas—the consent of the governed through popular vote, public education and welfare, economic development, environmental and market regulation—was firmly established in Lyme a century before the Declaration of Independence was signed. While universal literacy and public education were unknown in colonies such as Virginia and Pennsylvania, Connecticut in general and Lyme in particular saw to the education of their citizens from the earliest days. This literate and informed populace created the basis for Lyme and Connecticut's civic life, which E. Benjamin Andrews called "the most delightful example of popular government in all history."

It was at the Lyme town meeting of January 1766 that the citizens of Lyme threw down the gauntlet against Britain and declared that "we have an inviolable right by the God of nature as well as by the English constitution, (Which is unalienable even by ourselves)" and "we are unalterable fixt to defend our aforesaid Rights and Immunities." The core belief of Lyme's citizens, from the settlement's first establishment in the days of Oliver Cromwell, was self-governance.

In 1776, the English colonies on the East Coast of North America declared their independence from Great Britain and, banding together, created a new nation based on the principle of representative democracy. The United States of America served as a catalyst for enlightenment philosophy, which soon overtook and overthrew the monarchs that ruled great nations and ushered in the modern age. While these ideas, such as "the rights of man" or "life, liberty, and the pursuit of happiness" shook the world over the course of the next two centuries, the citizens of Lyme did not have to change their civic ways with the founding of the new nation. Indeed, when the Declaration of Independence was read on July 4, 1776, the democratic institutions of Lyme were already over 110 years old and on solid footing. Rather than Lyme needing to conform to the new order, the new order was just catching up with Lyme.

4

A PAIR OF SWASHBUCKLING YARNS

Rogers Lake is a sprawling body of water covering some 260 acres shared by the towns of Lyme and Old Lyme. What is it about the placid waters of this beloved lake that leads to speculation about pirates? Ask about the history of Rogers Lake at a gathering of locals, and, inevitably, someone will mention pirates or piracy or a secret cache of pirate treasure hidden nearby—though no one seems to know exactly where. Among these fanciful tales is one that says the lake itself was named for the infamous skull and crossbones flag that became known as the "Jolly Roger," and that by calling it "Rogers Lake," the pirates were claiming it as their own under their colors or flag.

The true origin of the name is far more mundane but interesting, nonetheless. Mark Lander of the Old Lyme Historical Society, who lived at Rogers Lake for many years, says:

> The Lake was once two separate ponds called Marvin's Pond and Rogers Pond. The northern pond was called Rogers Pond, after the Rogers family. There is an old house on Grassy Hill Road with a plaque indicating that it was once the Rogers house. As the house is not on the lake per se, it is likely that Rogers was a large landowner with land running to the pond. Marvin's Pond was named for the Reynold Marvin family in Laysville. In the 1670s, a dam was constructed at the southern end of Marvin's Pond which raised the water level enough to create one lake, first called the Great Pond and later Rogers Lake. The dam was built to impound water for the

mills downstream on Mill Brook. This brook makes the Lake one of the headwaters of the Lieutenant River. Halfway along the length of the lake the water is fairly shallow at a place called the Narrows. This is probably the separation point of the two ponds. The water there is shallow enough that in dry weather, it's possible to hit bottom with your boat motor if you're not careful. Supposedly there are the remains of stone walls on the lake bottom near this point. Successive wooden dams built to capture water to power mills, starting about 1672, started to raise the water level.

So, there you have it. No pirate flags, just a prominent landowner and some mill dams. But that doesn't explain the persistent legend of a buccaneer's booty buried at or near the lake. These tales have been passed down through the years and embellished with new details. An 1876 *Harper's Magazine* article noted that the Rogers Lake area "abounds in legends. When piracy was at its zenith, several noted brigands currently reported that Captain Kidd has buried a box of treasures under [an] overhanging 'bowlder.'"

Folklorist Charles M. Skinner added some spice to this tale, writing in 1896 that "a part of [Kidd's] treasure is under guard of a demon that springs upon intruders unless they recite scripture while digging for the money."

In 1906, George S. Roberts wrote about Rogers Lake in *Historic Towns of the Connecticut River Valley*, "It is tradition, that the cave, near Lion Rock, was

ROGERS LAKE FROM THE DAM, OLD LYME, CONN

Rogers Lake from the dam. *Old Lyme Historical Society Archive.*

a hiding place for Kidd and other pirates and that they buried treasure on the shores of the lake."

Since then, many people have speculated as to the locations of the famous cave and Lion (or Lion's) Rock. Wick Griswold included this tale in *Connecticut Pirates and Privateers* but sensibly pointed out that Lion's Rock was most likely named for Lion Gardner, a military engineer charged with building the fortifications at Saybrook and who later settled on the island that bears his name.

Hence, the elusive Lion Rock was probably located somewhere in the Long Island Sound or along the Connecticut River. Captain William Kidd was said to have had a base in the Thimble Islands, the archipelago located in and around the harbor of Stony Creek off the southeast coast of Branford, and it is worth noting that one of the largest Thimbles is called Rogers Island. Perhaps a case of mistaken geonomenclature? As Rogers Lake has no direct access to open water, it seems a bit unlikely that a band of pirates would choose it as the place to bury their hoard. But there are those who insist to this day that "X marks the spot" somewhere along the lakeside, and good luck to them in their quest.

Adding to the piratical mystique is the mysteriously named Blood Street. Curious sightseers taking a drive around the lake will eventually find themselves on Blood Street, possibly the most curiously named thoroughfare in Lyme–Old Lyme. Blood Street runs several miles between Bill Hill Road and Grassy Hill Road, ending at the intersection with Grassy Hill Road near the northern end of Rogers Lake.

This unusual street name has spawned many legends throughout the years and has lent a somewhat swashbuckling aura to one local organization— the Blood Street Sculls, Lyme–Old Lyme's rowing club. The rowers are a familiar sight on the lake, gliding swiftly through the water in their slender racing shells. The group's logo features a blood-red skull and crossed oars, and members are often asked about the origins of the name. The simple explanation is that the club's original boathouse was located on Blood Street off Rogers Lake, and the oars used in racing boats are, of course, called "sculls." But the origin of the street name itself remains clouded in mystery.

The Blood Street Sculls club was founded in 1967, and its early papers relate the legend that Blood Street supposedly owed its name to a local family who was known for stealing livestock. Apparently, the thieves were "not very careful in their butchering practices, which resulted in a trail of blood down the street, alerting their neighbors to their dishonest deeds." This story was repeated in a 1977 *Gazette* article, which named the purported livestock

The original Blood Street Sculls boathouse on Blood Street. *Old Lyme Historical Society Archive.*

thief as one Abenaijah Bill, without further supporting details. Some other speculations include a murder, possibly of a Marthe Rogers, who died in 1793; a Native American massacre; or discord among early feuding settlers, but none of these have been proven.

Mark Lander recalled asking the late Lyme historian Hiram Maxim III about these Blood Street stories and said that Maxim concluded the "best answer was that there had been a slaughterhouse there at one time." Maxim determined that there had never been a family named Blood living in the area nor had there ever been a battle with Native Americans nearby. These points lend weight to the slaughterhouse theory.

A 1999 article in the *Hartford Courant* said that name Blood Street did not appear on town land records until the latter half of the nineteenth century, and it was known previously as "Cross Road." It also cited Maxim, who said, "The area where the road is located in the southern section of Lyme was home to many sheep farms from Colonial times into the early 20th century. After the sheep were slaughtered, the farmers carried the carcasses on carts and wagons for sale at markets in Lyme and nearby towns. Maxim said the blood from the sheep that dripped off the wagons onto the road led to the road being named Blood Street sometime in the late 19th century."

Today, Rogers Lake is home to a new boathouse, named for Fred L. Emerson, a former Lyme resident who is considered the Father of Connecticut Rowing. The boathouse is owned by the Town of Old Lyme, and the Old Lyme Rowing Association (OLRA) operates several community rowing programs there, including the Lyme–Old Lyme High School Crew and the Blood Street Sculls, which moved from its Blood Street location to the more modern facility at Hains Park. OLRA was established in 1983 to support the sport of rowing in the shoreline area. Hains Park, on the southwest shore of Rogers Lake, was dedicated in 1961 and named for Paul W. Hains, a retired navy captain, who was first selectman of Old Lyme from 1953 to 1961. Hains had overseen the town's purchase of the land after a tragic fire in 1956 that destroyed the popular Lake Breeze Inn, and just a few days after Hains's death, residents voted to name the new Town Park after him.

5

DEAR OLD GOLDEN RULE DAYS

The tradition of public education in the Lymes is older than the republic itself. Because the town has always understood the inherent value of an educated, literate population, the formal teaching of reading, writing and arithmetic to Lyme's children has been the topic of town meetings since 1680. As proof of this dedication, the town itself funded a portion of the education budget, and the parents of all children, regardless of their attendance at school, were obligated to pay their portion of those expenses as well.

In 1644, the Connecticut Colony passed an educational decree, which was then revised and incorporated into the Code of 1650. These laws stated that any town of fifty families must appoint a teacher to instruct children to read and write, and any town of one hundred households must establish a school and hire a teacher well qualified to prepare youths for college. These laws included provisions not just for children but also for apprentices and servants.

In 1667, Lyme became an incorporated town of thirty families, which was well under the required number of fifty households to support a schoolmaster, so in the earliest days, lessons were given at home. By 1680, Lyme had grown to approximately sixty families, and in March of that year, it was decided "at a metting of the Townsmen to consider the prudentialls of the Towne—and particularly being ordered by the Towne to appoynt and Judg who are needful and fitting to go to Schole and so may pay the three pounds ordered to the schoolmaster and having seriously considered the matter and doe find that all wch are capable of receiving benefit by the said schole and not sent accordingly, wee doe therefore apoynt that as well as wch doe not goe as they doe go shall pay…"

There follows a list of townspeople with school-age children (all boys) and the amount each family would be expected to pay. William Measure was selected as schoolmaster, and at the same meeting, it was decided to hire "two school dames" to instruct Lyme's "young children and maids to read, and to do whatever else they are capable of doing, either knitting or sewing." It may be noted that Mr. Measure received six pounds, five shillings for his work, while the "dames" were given just forty shillings each. These dame schools were the one kept near Duck River by the "Widow Waller" and another located "Between the Rivers."

At a time when illiteracy was the norm, most Connecticut citizens could read and write. In *History of the United States*, E. Benjamin Andrews notes that even in the mid-1700s "schools were almost unknown" in Virginia, while "in popular education, New England led not only the continent but the world." In the vanguard were Massachusetts and Connecticut, where early settlers believed the ability to read and write was essential to "keeping the devil at bay."

It was expected that each person should be able to read the Bible and interpret the scriptures for themselves. May Hall James, in her authoritative *Educational History of Old Lyme*, emphasizes this point, stating, "Being able to read the Bible in English, was seen as necessary to one's salvation. Men, women, children and even slaves and servants were expected to know their catechism. This was seen as necessary to keeping order in a civilized community."

The terms of the school year fluctuated according to the needs of weather and harvest. The shortest term was three months and the longest was nine months, with breaks in the schedule when all hands were needed for farm work and other necessary tasks.

The number of schoolhouses grew with the town itself, and in 1806, the Black Hall District School was established as follows:

We the subscribers agree to build a school house for the 8th school district in the First Society of Lyme of the following description viz, to be 17 feet in length and 14 feet in width in the clear, and 7 and a half feet between joints to be covered with pine boards as high as the desks and plastered with lime mortar above and over head—to have 3 windows and the outside door to open into an entry by the side of the chimney, and a closet on the other side of the chimney—the house to be placed on the parade where the two roads meet on the District—and we agree to defray the expense of the house in proportions annexed to our names respectively.

1ˢᵗ December 1806. Lee Lay one eighth, John Griswold one eighth, Matthew Griswold one quarter, Roger Griswold one third, Diodati J. Griswold one eighth.

Black Hall Traditions and Reminiscences by Adeline Bartlett Allyn states the above was read to a festive crowd gathered for the school's one hundredth anniversary in 1906. The day was celebrated with much pomp and circumstance, including cake, speeches and "a parade where the two roads meet."

Private schools also thrived in Old Lyme. Many were schools for girls taught by educated women as a respectable way to contribute to the family purse. In the 1830s, Phoebe Griffin Noyes's husband Daniel added a schoolroom and accommodations for students in their house.

South Lyme Schoolhouse, 1921. *Old Lyme Historical Society Archive.*

Boxwood Manor, Old Lyme, 1905. *Old Lyme Historical Society Archive.*

Phoebe had studied painting and French in New York City and taught art in addition to reading, writing and sums. The Lyme Academy, a college preparatory school, was located at the corner of Lyme Street and Academy Lane. It was destroyed by a fire in the mid-1860s, but the street name remains. Florence Griswold, her mother and sisters opened a school in their home in 1878, with a focus on music, and in 1890, Mrs. Richard Sill Griswold started a school at her Lyme Street manse known as "Boxwood."

In 1855, the town of Lyme was divided along the old First and North Society lines. The First Society was incorporated as South Lyme and quickly renamed Old Lyme. In the 1860 census, the population of Old Lyme is approximately 1,300. Old Lyme's eight school districts are shown on Beers's 1868 map: Center, Neck, Sill, Laysville, Between-the-Rivers, Mile Creek, Four Mile River and Black Hall. May Hall James says these districts reflected the ones that had been laid out in 1783. She then details the emergence of new Connecticut public school laws in the 1860s that abolished the system of district schools. Teachers were recruited and trained in the new system, and in 1871, an education convention was held at Hartford. The State Board of Education was given authority to issue teaching certificates and ensure that teachers were uniformly qualified.

With the dawning of the twentieth century, the educational system in the Lymes began to more closely resemble the one we have today, with certified teachers and exams for students to measure progress. In 1914, *The Connecticut School Register* decreed:

> *All parents and those who have care of children shall bring them up in some lawful and honest employment and instruct them or cause them to be instructed in reading, writing, spelling, English grammar, geography, arithmetic and US History. Every parent or other person having control of a child over seven and under sixteen years of age shall cause such child to attend public day school regularly....No child under 14 years of age shall be employed at any time in any mechanical, mercantile or manufacturing establishment.*

In East Lyme, the early school best known to us today is the "Little Boston School." According to the East Lyme Historical Society, it was founded in 1734 by order of the governor and located "halfway between the Thomas Lee house and the Quality Smith house" on land given by Thomas Lee.

The district of Little Boston was named because it had aspirations toward being a "center of learning and culture." The school taught the basics of reading, writing and arithmetic but also Latin, Greek, astronomy and other sciences. The first schoolmaster was Samuel Comstock, whose son (and pupil) went on to an illustrious career as a doctor of medicine and author of scientific tomes. The school was closed in 1922 and is now owned by the East Lyme Historical Society, which moved it onto the grounds of the Thomas Lee house, where it stands today.

East Lyme was incorporated in 1839, setting itself off from Lyme and becoming its own town. It had nine school districts: Niantic, Niantic Hill, Flanders Village, Walnut Hill, Black Point, Head of the River, Mack's Mill, Toad Rock and Little Boston. As East Lyme's population grew, larger schools were needed. Olive Tubbs Chendali tells of the building of Niantic Center School in 1928 to accommodate the post–World War I baby boom and lists herself as among its first graduates. Students either went to private schools or to public high school in New London until the post–World War II baby boom necessitated that East Lyme build its own high school.

In Lyme, before the opening of the Consolidated School in 1934, the town had been divided into individual school districts by neighborhood. Schoolhouses were located in Hadlyme, Grassy Hill, Brockway, Pleasant Valley, Bill Hill and Sterling City. These were one-room schoolhouses with

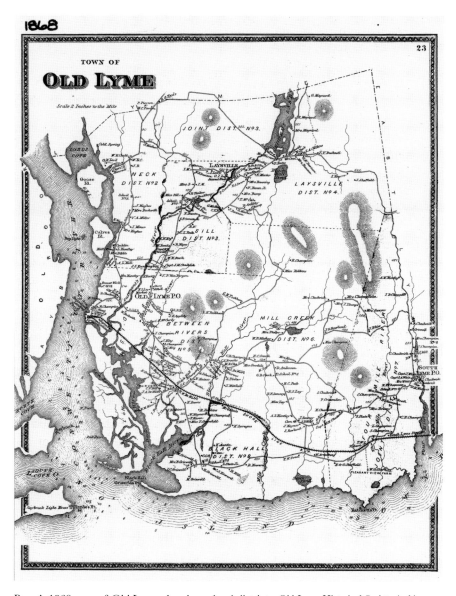

Beers's 1868 map of Old Lyme showing school districts. *Old Lyme Historical Society Archive.*

Old Lyme Central School, 1913. *Old Lyme Historical Society Archive.*

Thomas Lee House and Little Boston Schoolhouse, 2019. *Michaelle Pearson.*

Parade, Bill Hill or Sterling Hill School, Lyme. *Lyme Public Hall and Local History Archives.*

grades one through eight sharing a single large classroom. Doris "Doad" Jewett of Lyme attended both the Sterling City and Brockway schools and later taught at the Sterling City schoolhouse. Her memoir, *Things Remembered*, recalls, "Each school had one room with a stove in the middle, a teacher's desk in front, and the children's desks in rows, the small ones in the front and they increased in size as they went down to the back. They were fastened to the floor, had an ink well and a shelf underneath for papers and books....The schoolhouses had no electricity, no plumbing, and no central heating."

Jewett goes on in detail, saying the schools had no running water, so water had to be fetched either from the closest well or from a nearby spring. Students brought tin cups to school and helped with stacking firewood into piles. The teacher had to arrive early in the morning to start the fire and was responsible for keeping the schoolroom neat and clean.

Today, the Lymes are still known for the excellent quality of their schools. Though the three towns have grown in very different ways, they all place great emphasis and a large percentage of their town budgets on supporting their schools. Lyme (population 2,400) and Old Lyme (population 7,500) share resources as Regional School District 18. Lyme and Old Lyme operate separate elementary schools, but students from both towns attend Lyme–Old Lyme Middle School and Lyme–Old Lyme High School. This allows the two small towns greater educational opportunities than would otherwise be possible in a smaller, single-town district. East Lyme, with a population approaching nearly 20,000 people, has a larger school system. Voters in all three towns today are as actively engaged in school politics and budgeting as their counterparts at those seventeenth-century town meetings.

6

Down by the Old Mill Stream

Driving south on I-95, it's obvious when you're entering the Lymes. The interstate suddenly twists and turns, the lanes narrow and, inevitably, there are traffic jams that stretch for miles. All too often there are horrific crashes—indeed, the stretch of interstate through the Lymes accounts for a quarter of all the state's serious accidents east of the Connecticut River. Built in the 1940s as the Blue Star Highway, a "Super-2" providing access to the new Baldwin Bridge, the road was never upgraded to interstate standards when it became part of the Connecticut Turnpike, and then I-95 in the late 1950s. The grades are too steep, the bridges too low, the shoulders meager or nonexistent. It carries nearly twice the traffic, and at much higher speeds, than it was designed to handle. With only two lanes in either direction, like so many other aspects of the Lymes, it's a relic from another era.

Unusual features abound along this ten-mile stretch of bad road. Entering East Lyme, it curls around a small graveyard at its southern perimeter, bends around the headwaters of the Niantic River at a place called "Golden Spur" and threads its way between one hill called "Oswegatchie" and another named "Sodom." Following the path of an old Indian trail, which became a colonial route called "the country road," the names of the exits give clues as to the history of the region. Four Mile River refers to a body of water four miles east of Lyme's first settlement at Black Hall. Society Road gets its name from Lyme's second Congregational Meeting House and parish, which eventually became the town of East Lyme. Oil Mill Road refers to a long-gone colonial-era industrial site, and Flanders gets its name from the numerous textile mills that once dotted Latimer's Brook. Indeed, a driver idling in a traffic jam might notice, just before the sign for Exit 74 to Niantic, a pond with a dam and waterfall by the southbound lane of the highway. Now the site of a small park with a fish ladder enabling alewives to access their spawning grounds where fresh water meets salt, this was once the water source that powered a mill owned by Moses Warren, a native son who fought in the Revolutionary War.

Looking at a map of the Lymes, you will see numerous lakes and ponds with small streams at either end. Most of these were once sites of mills established at the very beginning of the colonial era, and even if the mills themselves are gone, traces of their activity remain in the landscape. The stonework dams that created the ponds have proven remarkably resilient, even as the ponds have been repurposed in various ways, from ice making and fishing to swimming and boating. The earliest mills were established in what is now the Silltown section of Old Lyme, and their history reflects a time when government and economy, two sectors that today are often seen as contradictory or hostile were then a unified expression of a community working to establish itself in a new land.

The earliest Lyme town meeting records give us detailed accounts of the region's economy, which was regulated, and sometimes even established, by the town itself. In 1676, the town commissioned William Waller and Reynold Marvin to build a gristmill on the Lieutenant River to grind the town's corn in exchange for eighty acres of arable upland and meadows. Waller and Marvin were briefly given a monopoly as millers. One year later, Thomas Lee was given land in exchange for building a sawmill on the Lieutenant, with a promise to saw the town's wood for seventeen pence per bundle cheaper than competitors in surrounding areas. A second sawmill was authorized in 1678, when Richard Ely was given liberty to dam the Falls River below Biggs Meadow, now the site of the Sterling City Cemetery in Lyme, as long as he allowed town inhabitants to saw their own wood at cheaper rates. In 1680, Abram Brounson was chosen to attend to the town's gristmill on the Lieutenant River, with the agreement that every Thursday he would grind all the corn brought to him by town residents. That same year, Joseph Peck, Edward DeWolfe and Richard Lord were given permission to build another sawmill—this one on the Eight Mile River. When the mills were in need of repair, the "trained band" or town militia was summoned, and each soldier would dedicate a day to patching the dam and fixing the mill.

Gristmills and sawmills represented two basic necessities: food and shelter. Soon, other enterprises, such as fulling mills for the processing of wool, were added to the mix. On Latimer's Brook in the eastern end of town, Peter Hackley was authorized to build a fulling mill in 1693. Philip Tabor ran the mill until 1741, and while it was briefly pressed into service as a sawmill, Moses Warren operated it as a fulling mill again in the early nineteenth century. Warren sold his mill in 1821. Upstream, other mills had been established, including a turning mill for the manufacture of implement handles and another gristmill. All but one of these mills on Latimer Brook are long gone.

Winding its way through a notch between the two-hundred-foot heights of Oswegatchie and Sodom Hill and joining the Niantic River at what was once called Wolf Pit Plain, and later Golden Spur—originally the site of a Nehantic fort—the brook has seen generations of development and redevelopment on its shores. The country road that followed its banks was improved in 1807 and became the Lyme and New London Turnpike. This widened, straightened and finely graded turnpike surveyed by Moses Warren soon assumed the status of primary road through the Lymes, superseding the old Post Road that ran along today's Route 156. In the twentieth century, the old turnpike became part of Route 1, the primary coastal road that runs from Maine to Florida. Running alongside Route 1, and sometimes over the old turnpike, Interstate 95 was established in the 1950s. The old colonial homes along Latimer's Brook, landmarks such as the Caulkins Tavern visited by both George Washington and the Marquis de Lafayette, and Moses Warren's home near the corner of the Turnpike and Chesterfield Road were torn down to make way for shopping centers. The Caulkins Tavern was razed in favor of a new McDonalds in the 1990s, and that McDonalds in turn was torn down a few years later to make way for the CVS drugstore on the corner of Routes 1 and 161. Throughout everything, the mill dam and pond from the first mill in 1693 improbably remain to this day, burbling reminders from the dawn of America's Industrial Age.

Continuing west down Route 1 from Flanders Four Corners in East Lyme, we come to the border of Old Lyme at the Four Mile River. The highway crosses the river at Plant's Dam, an area named after the industrial magnate Mortimer Plant, who once owned choice properties along the Connecticut coast and briefly operated a trolley line serving the Lymes. The dam at this portion of the river precedes Mortimer Plant by quite a few years, however, as town meeting records mention a sawmill at this site as early as 1716. Taking a left at Four Mile River Road and heading south, just before the

Caulkins Tavern, circa 1940. *WPA/Connecticut State Library.*

intersection of Four Mile River and the old Post Road, now called Shore Road or Route 156, the traveler can see a rough stonework dam with a millpond behind the houses on the east side of the road. This was the site of a mill built by Thomas Waite in 1716, which alternately served as a sawmill and corn mill for over a century and a half.

Along with stonework, place names provide clues to long-vanished enterprises. Macks Mill Hill in East Lyme is named after William Mack, who dammed the Pattagansett River and established his gristmill there in the eighteenth century. In 1785, Joshua Powers bought the mill from Mack, and the millpond, to this day, is known as Powers Lake. It is interesting to note that both Mack and Powers are listed in Moses Warren's roll of slaves as slaveholders, with Mack owning an eleven-year-old by the name of Jack and Powers a twenty-year-old named Frank.

By the mid-nineteenth century, Lyme's industries included distilleries, iron furnaces and gun manufacturers, along with cotton, oil, powder, paper, grist, and sawmills. The area surrounding Mill Creek, between Rogers Lake and the Lieutenant River in Old Lyme, became a manufacturing hub, with an 1810 map showing a satinet factory, gristmill and fuller's mill. The most iconic mill in the Lymes that still stands is the old stone building known as the Bradbury Mill. Built by Captain Thomas Sill and Deacon Nathaniel

Lower Mill Pond at Four Mile River, 2019. *Jim Lampos.*

Maston in the early nineteenth century and later purchased by Oliver Lay, the stone mill became a celebrated woolen mill under James Bradbury in the late nineteenth century. It fabricated "satinet cloth for men's apparel," fine woolens and other materials. To power the increasingly busy mill, Rogers Lake was dammed in 1822, and a mill chase was extended down Mill Creek. The 1822 dam was purchased by the Town of Old Lyme in 1922, and apart from some patchwork and a new timber gate in 1976, the old dam remained in service until 2013, when it was completely rebuilt just nine years shy of its two hundredth birthday.

Hydropower, which made Lyme's industries possible, was also part of its undoing. Until the 1830s, economic activities were primarily local enterprises. Each town had its own small mills to serve the community, and those mills had to be close to navigable waterways for raw materials, such as timber, to be shipped to them. Towns that were landlocked or didn't have navigable rivers were at a disadvantage, as materials would have had to be hauled overland by horse or oxen. It was a slow, taxing enterprise. One new technology changed all that: steam.

Bradbury's Mill, 2019. *Jim Lampos.*

Bradbury's Mill Dam in Spring by Edward Francis Rook. *UCONN CT Digital Archive, New Britain Museum of Art.*

Steam begat the railroad, and by the 1840s, railroads were winding their way up riverbanks to the interior of the countryside, opening areas that were previously inaccessible and allowing large mills to be built along shallow, swift-moving rivers that would provide ample power. While the rivers weren't conducive to transport, they didn't need to be anymore. The train would take care of that, carrying raw materials to the mill and loading out finished goods, which it could then transport to any part of the nation.

By the time the railroad came to the Lymes in 1851, the towns of the interior, such as Norwich, Willimantic and Worcester, were already becoming major industrial hubs with large factories that provided an economy of scale unimaginable in Old Lyme. Adding to the insult, waterpower in the Lymes was not a consistently reliable source. The *Connecticut Eastern News* reported in 1894 that "it has become necessary for Bradbury's upper mill to be shut down owing to the extreme scarcity of water. The lower mill is running only half time. This is very unfortunate for just the time as the firm is crowded with orders and could run ten hours a day six days a week." The mill remained closed for much of October.

As the twentieth century progressed, manufacturing in the Lymes continued to diminish, and the mills became only a memory. The advances in technology that led to Lyme's decline allowed mill towns to sprout up all along the Shetucket and Quinnebaug River Valleys. Those towns in turn would lose their industries to the Carolinas in the mid-1950s, when electric power and interstates meant that factories could be located anywhere and didn't need a source of hydropower or railroad access. Industrialists in search of cheap, non-union labor in the South abandoned New England almost completely by the 1970s, leaving a wake of economic devastation from which many once-proud Yankee mill towns are still struggling to recover. In the 1990s, the South lost most of those mills to Mexico and South America and, shortly thereafter, to China and other Asian nations that didn't have the inconveniences of labor and environmental law. So, the cycle goes.

Meanwhile, Lyme slowly found a new purpose. Though it had lost much of its population, the natural beauty of the town did not escape the notice of urban dwellers, and the charms of the land that time forgot drew artists from New York's Art Students League, who arrived in the summer months to paint the town's iconic scenes, not the least of which were Mill Creek and Bradbury's Mill.

7

THE PERIPATETIC LIBRARIES

Today we think of lending libraries as an essential part of our communities, and in the early days of the Lymes, people felt much the same way. Literacy and book learning were held in high esteem, and books were an expensive and highly coveted commodity. Anyone fortunate enough to own a book or two soon found they could lend their treasures to fellow bibliophiles in exchange for new reading material.

In 1701, the Collegiate Library was started by a group of ministers who pooled some of their books in hopes of creating a school in Saybrook after the manner of Harvard. When the college that would become known as Yale was eventually founded, the location chosen was not Saybrook or Lyme but New Haven. The school expected that the "books belonging to the college" would be brought to New Haven, which did not sit well with the original donors. Constables were sent to transport the books, but angry citizens overturned the carts, unyoked the oxen and created scenes of general mayhem to prevent the them from being taken. Order was eventually restored, but this "Battle of the Books" resulted in some 250 volumes missing from the inventory that arrived at the college.

In 1737, a circulating library was shared among the four towns of Lyme, Guilford, Killingworth and Saybrook—an area encompassing today's Lyme, Old Lyme, East Lyme, Old Saybrook, Deep River, Killingworth, Chester, Guilford, Madison, Clinton and Westbrook. In this innovative system, volumes were auctioned off to readers each month when the portable library arrived in town with its shelves strapped to the back of a donkey.

The books were due approximately one month in the future, when the cart made its return circuit. Shares in this "Four-Town Library" could be sold or transferred by members. A speech given at the opening of the Old Lyme–Phoebe Griffin Noyes Library in 1898 noted that by 1787, the Four-Town Library possessed "60 folios, 24 quartos and 307 other volumes having a total value of £167.7s." Many of the books dealt with subjects of divinity or religious philosophy, but there were also several "volumes of travel, and three novels: *Amelia*, *Sir Charles Grandison*, and *Don Quixote*."

After the dissolution of the Four-Town Library in 1790, Reverend David Higgins of the North Society Congregational Church in Lyme started a library at his home, subscribed to by thirty-eight other men, who each contributed to the cost of purchasing books. The Lyme Public Hall hosted an exhibit, *Libraries of Lyme*, in 2013, which featured this library, stating that its books included "not only sermons and religious tracts but books on farming, geography, history and etiquette, along with a book that is generally considered the first American novel: *The Power of Sympathy*" by William Hill Brown. Also of note in Lyme was the small lending library established at the home of John White Bill on Bill Hill and the Joshuatown Union Sewing Society's collection of circulating books funded by the sale of sewing projects. The society was a group of men and women founded with the ideal of "acquiring and diffusing knowledge, and to avoid in every form sectarianism and bigotry." To this end, it lent books to members and other readers willing to pay "a returnable deposit and small reading charge."

Old Lyme also had several different groups that emerged to fill the gap left after the Four-Town Library was dissolved and before the opening of the new library in 1898. In 1816, the Female Reading Society began meeting weekly in ladies' homes on or near present-day Lyme Street for the stated purpose of "reading from the holy scriptures and any other book whose tendency is to elevate the mind and improve the heart." Many of the town's prominent women were listed as members, including both Phoebe Lord (who hosted the society's first meeting) and her daughter, Phoebe Griffin Noyes.

In the 1870s, Douglas Waite (brother of Supreme Court justice Morrison Waite) formed the "Lyme Book Club," which later bequeathed its books to the Ladies' Library Society. Dry, accessible storage space was at a premium, so the ladies housed their books in various locations around town. In *For the Love of Books*, Alma Merry Tatum describes the journey of the collection from "George Babcock's tin shop, on Lyme Street, across from the current library" to the "small building that still stands on the corner of Ferry and Neck Roads, known as the "Band Room," as it provided rehearsal and storage space for the town band. Tatum says, "patrons who found the roads too muddy could also drop their books off at Champion's Store, on the corner of Lyme Street and Ferry Road."

Evelyn MacCurdy Salisbury wrote in 1892 that the Ladies' Library Society possessed "about 2,500 bound volumes, besides about 3,500 books and pamphlets which are unbound." Mrs. Salisbury was an educational pioneer and philanthropist, who alternately offered to donate a home for a town library and/or an academy school. In 1895, the Ladies' Library Society incorporated as the Ladies' Library Association, with Elizabeth Griswold as its first president, and expressed concern that MacCurdy's proffered site was neither fireproof nor centrally located. Evelyn MacCurdy Salisbury quickly took umbrage at this and withdrew her offer in an impassioned open letter to the *Sound Breeze* newspaper.

The library project soon found a new benefactor in Charles H. Ludington. Ludington was a wealthy merchant from New York and was married to Phoebe Griffin Noyes's daughter Josephine. The new library was to be situated on the site of Phoebe's birthplace, the old Lord homestead, which had been donated by the Lord family for the purpose. The new library building was designed in the Colonial Revival style by Ernest Greene, and work proceeded quickly. The foundation was dug in December 1897, and construction proceeded at a rapid pace. On June 23, 1898, the building was formally dedicated in a ceremony honoring its namesake, artist and teacher Phoebe Griffin Noyes, and simultaneously securing Ludington's local fame as best son-in-law ever.

The history of the East Lyme Library is a bit less dramatic but no less important and still quite peripatetic. The town of East Lyme was incorporated in 1839, and according to the East Lyme Public Library, its first library was founded in 1888 by sixty-five founding members. This was known as the Niantic Library and Reading Room Association and met at Union Hall, or Luce Hall, on Pennsylvania Avenue. In 1897, it was formally incorporated as the Niantic Public Library Association. Dues were $1.00 per year or $0.50 for summer residents. Between 1899 and 1920, the library changed locations several times in rented or shared spaces, including St. John's Episcopal Church and "branches" at many of the schools in town, until a new public library was constructed on Main Street and dedicated in 1921.

The library's fireplace was completed in 1925 and was built of stones from the 1831 Old Stone Church, which had been quarried by Samuel Smith in Oswegatchie Hills. The church was demolished in 1879. There

Niantic Library fireplace built of stones from the Old Stone Church. *East Lyme Historical Society.*

were additions to the building in 1966 and 1979. In 1977, the library was renamed the "East Lyme Public Library." In 1990, the library moved into the town's new $7.5 million community services complex. The old library building on Main Street in Niantic now houses the Children's Museum, but the historic granite fireplace is no longer visible, as it was covered by drywall during renovations.

Today, Lyme, Old Lyme and East Lyme all have beautiful, modern libraries that retain a sense of the past. The East Lyme and Lyme libraries have incorporated space for their respective historical societies' archives, and the Old Lyme–Phoebe Griffin Noyes Library has preserved the original 1898 building as a reading room, with subsequent additions to provide space and flexibility for contemporary programming needs. Just as in the earliest days, these libraries are places where people gather to read, discuss and learn.

8

A SURVEY OF MOSES WARREN

I n reading Lyme histories, some names keep turning up. One in particular makes a reader question whether it could possibly be the same person in each instance. He was a Revolutionary War veteran, Lyme selectman, master of the Pythagoras Masonic Lodge, turnpike commissioner, justice of the peace, probate court judge, overseer of the Nehantic Indians, mill owner, presidential elector and representative to the General Assembly of Connecticut. Is it possible that a singular Moses Warren played all of these roles? Certainly. It was, after all, the age of the Renaissance Man. But there's also a Moses Warren who was a famed cartographer and surveyor of Cleveland, Ohio, with a town named after him in the Buckeye State. That couldn't possibly be the same Moses Warren, could it? Indeed, it could. At the turn of the nineteenth century in Lyme, not only did every road seem to lead to Moses Warren's door, but it was also very likely that he surveyed each of those roads himself.

Born in 1762 and a descendent of Mayflower pilgrim Richard Warren, Moses Warren Jr. grew up in Lyme and was educated in the East Society's public school. His father, Moses Warren Sr., was a veteran of the French and Indian War, fought at Ticonderoga and was a captain in the Continental army. It was natural, then, that in the pivotal year of 1776, at the age of fourteen, Moses Warren Jr. would leave school and join his father in the Revolutionary cause. The young Moses started as a messenger in the militia and by 1779, at the age of seventeen, had become an orderly sergeant in the fourth company of the third regiment of the Connecticut infantry.

By the war's conclusion, he had risen to the rank of lieutenant and was a distinguished member of Lyme society.

Admitted as a freeman of the state by John Lay Esq. in 1786, Moses Warren Jr. was elected to the Lyme Board of Selectmen in the following year. The twenty-five-year-old Warren was an ambitious man. He was already engaged in a partnership with Job and Samuel Taber in a sawmill operation and, by 1789, was building a mill of his own—a fulling mill on the Pattagansett River, which he would own and operate for the next thirty-five years. Engaged in all aspects of building and operating the mill, Warren first traveled to Hartford to observe the operation of similar mills. With this knowledge in hand, he returned to Lyme to source the wood and build the wheel for the mill himself. On June 29, 1789, with the help of twenty-five to thirty neighbors, Warren raised the forty-two-by-sixteen-and-a-half-foot mill and provided one gallon of New England rum one and a half gallons of West Indian rum to the crew, making the labor more joyful.

Fulling mills processed raw sheep's wool, carding and whitening the product to make it ready for manufacture into cloth. Fuller's earth, a natural clay, was used in the process, thus giving this type of mill its name. The

Site of Moses Warren's Fulling Mill, 2019. *Jim Lampos.*

wool was placed in hot water with Fuller's earth, which stripped the wool of lanolin and grease. The wool was also dyed in the mill, and Warren wrote of his first experiments with the dyeing process in January 1790. It is remarkable to see the degree to which manufacturing was an organic process at the very dawn of the Industrial Age. In making the color "bottle green," Warren first gathered alder and sumac and "set the kettle" with it. He let it sit for three days, and then added fustic, alum and a compound of oil vitriol and indigo. Once that brew was set, he added copperas, an old name for ferrous sulfate, a salt compound still used medicinally today but at that time it was also used as a dye fixative. His first experiments failed, resulting in black cloth, but with trial and error, Warren soon learned how to consistently make the elusive bottle green color that was so favored by the fashionistas of the day.

Like all mills at that time, Warren's was powered by natural means—animal or human muscle, wind or, in this case, water. Several mills were built in the Flanders area of Lyme at the headwaters of the Niantic River, and for the most part, the mill owners lived close by. Unlike today, when factory ownership may be a faceless corporation on the other side of the planet, the mill owners of the early Industrial Revolution lived near their operations and workers and were part of the community. Moses Warren lived just a stone's throw from his mill in the Red House he inherited from his father, which stood just south of Flanders Four Corners. Directly across the road was the home of his friend Dr. Daniel Caulkins.

Daniel Caulkins was the physician who attended to the young Moses when he was inoculated against smallpox on April 4, 1777, at the home of Esquire Lee. The project of inoculating Connecticut soldiers against smallpox was overseen by another Lyme patriot Major General Samuel Holden Parsons. The treatment involved infecting patients with a small dose of smallpox, which rendered them ill for a period of time but helped them build an immunity, allowing them to avoid a more serious case of the often-fatal disease. The treatment was still controversial at the time, but it was supported by Benjamin Franklin and mandated by George Washington, and it proved successful in mitigating the spread of smallpox, which had been so devastating to the ranks of American troops.

Moses Warren was ill for twenty-four days after inoculation and was quarantined in a hospital. It proved to be one of the most important periods in his life. Rather than idling his time recovering from the illness, Warren used this otherwise fallow period to begin his study of arithmetic and geometry. Self-taught in these disciplines, he soon became an expert surveyor. In 1786, he was appointed highway surveyor for the Town of Lyme and the next year

Pages from Moses Warren's journal. *East Lyme Historical Society.*

for the County of New London. His skills were noted by the authorities in the state capitol, and in 1796, he was given an assignment that altered the course of his life. He was sent to Ohio—to the land Connecticut claimed before the Revolution—and along with Moses Cleveland, grandfather of President Grover Cleveland, he was charged with surveying and laying out the area in and around what would come to be known as Cleveland, Ohio.

Warren's letters to his wife, Mehitable, from 1796 to 1797 give insight into the challenges the surveyor faced in the virgin wilderness of Ohio. These were not inconsiderable, as Samuel Holden Parsons, who had been sent there to administer those territories ten years earlier, was killed in a canoe accident while surveying the same territory. Warren's early letters home were full of promise and adventure, opening with the salutation "Dearest" and closing with "yours till Death." They tell of hearing panthers at night and eating rattlesnake chowder to survive. From the forks of the Cuyahoga River he talks of finding a settlement of two or three families and "the first white woman I have seen in 51 days." He talks of news that the Spaniards were attempting to entice Native American tribes to attack the settlements and his camps, but Warren writes that "the Indians are more afraid of us than we are of them."

His notes on the native tribes of Ohio paint a picture of a land and people on the cusp of the modern world—still living in their traditional ways but increasingly coming in contact with settlers from the other side of the Appalachians who are bringing with them the ways of a new nation, economy and social order. Warren notes the similarity of these tribes in custom and language to the natives of Connecticut and speculates that they may be closely related. He has confidence that he can soon learn their language and finds it easy to bond with them. He writes, "I have seen Tawa Warriors when they first came in sight of our camp shake like one with an ague, and one peaceable word and good natured look dispel it all and make them composedly light their pipes." Smoking the calumet or peace pipe sealed the treaties that Cleveland and Warren signed with tribes they encountered along the way, exchanging wampum, jewelry, paint and whisky for settlement rights.

Surviving illness and dangers from exposure to the elements, Warren became more distant and formal in his letters to his wife as his year and a half away from home grinds on. Instead of the "Dearest" of his 1796 letters, his 1797 letters begin with "Madame" and sign off with the poetic but formal, "until that Stroke of Time that shall finish the Existence of one us." In his last letter before his return, he writes on November 28, 1787, that he hopes to be home by Christmas, and "when this tiresome business is off my hands I will urge my way eastward to the Rocky hills of Niantic and as a consolation will add that I do not as yet calculate to undertake this kind of business again."

Though he resolved to never again wander the wilderness blazing trails, he was moved to compose a poem upon his departure from the "west." In his "Explorer's Farewell," he waxes rhapsodic about the virtues of this new land, where the outmoded mores and narrow-mindedness of hidebound New England could be left behind:

> But when yon journey leave behind
> The bigot's stern unsocial mind
> On sterile stone hills
> These Western lands are far too good
> To cherish such a rankling brood
> The worst of human ills.

He was perhaps one of the first American poets to celebrate the promise of the West:

The sciences do not forget
But then transplant and cultivate
By precept and example
Till western students shall out do
The schools of Yale and Harvard, too
And on the pendants trample.

Though Warren was clearly conflicted by the allure of the unwritten West versus the comforts of his native soil, whether the rocky hills of Niantic were the alluring and attractive beacons of home or the repulsive, "sterile" refuge of the "bigot's stern unsocial mind," return to Niantic he did, though not without first leaving his indelible mark on Ohio. From Cleveland streets named for his geometric hero Euclid to the burgh bearing his name, the survey and plan Warren laid out more than two centuries ago still organizes the steps of today's inhabitants on Lake Erie's shore.

Back home, Warren continued applying the skills he had honed in the West, surveying turnpikes such as the Lyme–New London Turnpike, today's Route 1, which ran past his fulling mill and home at Flanders. He also became commissioner of Niantic Bridge and various turnpike authorities, such as the Guilford and Durham. He was elected to various offices, including representative to the general assembly. All of these honors would

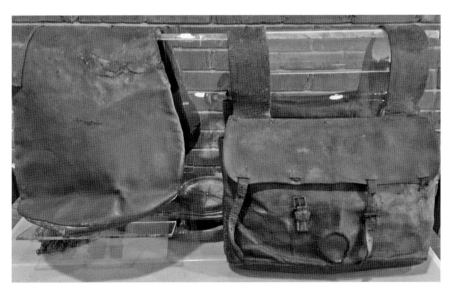

Moses Warren's saddlebags and surveying tools displayed at East Lyme Town Hall. *Michaelle Pearson.*

have been lost to the mists of time had he not drafted a document that has proved invaluable to anyone seeking to understand Lyme's past: the 1811 Warren Map of Lyme's First Society. This map, which essentially depicts what is today's Old Lyme, is not only remarkably accurate for its day, but it's also instantly recognizable, save for the interstate, railroad and suburban-style subdivisions. More importantly, he lists all of the prominent features of the landscape and identifies the houses and owners. As such, it continues to serve as an invaluable document, and the first thing a curious student of Lyme's history encounters is the Warren Map—a worthy plan for the beginning of a fascinating journey. Working on a broader scale, with George Gillet, he drafted a map of the state of Connecticut that same year, which provided an unprecedented level of accurate detail.

Living to the venerable age of seventy-three, Moses Warren in his later years accumulated laurels of recognition as one of Connecticut's most revered citizens. He had the privilege of greeting Lafayette in Lyme with Masonic honors and escorting him along the turnpike he had surveyed from the banks of the Connecticut River to the Caulkins Tavern at the head of the Niantic. Inspired by Lafayette, in 1825 Warren served on a committee to construct a monument at the Revolutionary War battlefield of Fort Griswold in Groton. It was Lafayette's admonition to the victorious troops at Yorktown to "remember New London," where the traitor Benedict Arnold had committed his most atrocious infamy. The committee, formed to create a lasting monument to the martyrs of the Groton massacre, was "assembled here to commemorate their glory and fate" and to "recommend to our fellow citizens the erecting of a Monument which shall remain to posterity as a witness of their gratitude, and perpetuate the memory of those who have sealed with their blood the liberties of their country; and the same shall be a memorial to our children forever." The committee was successful on all counts, and the monument still stands as a memento of sacrifice and a beloved symbol of the spirit of the Connecticut shore.

Warren remained active to the end. At age sixty-five, he was appointed to survey the disputed boundary between the State of Connecticut and the Commonwealth of Massachusetts. The work of the three-member committee was decisive, and that border remains true to this day. On May 4, 1831, he was cited in the record of the general assembly when "the House was called to order at 10 o'clock by Moses Warren, Esq., of Lyme, he being the oldest member present."

While his maps and legacy remain, it is difficult to find physical traces of Moses Warren's world today. His family home just south of Flanders Four

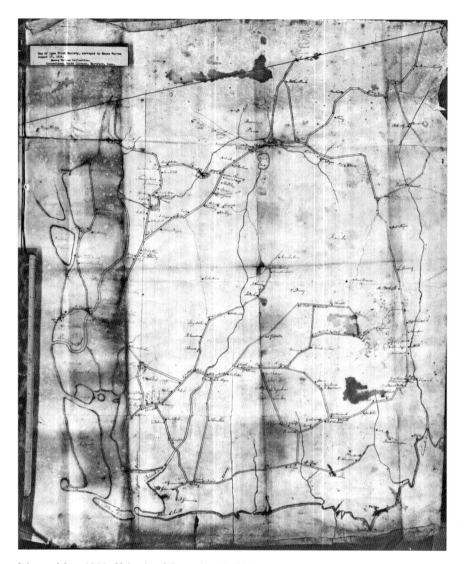

Warren Map, 1811. *University of Connecticut MAGIC map server.*

Corners survived until 1968 but was torn down to make way for a strip mall. Indeed, hardly anything remains of Warren's world at Flanders Four Corners, except the ruins of his dam, the mill's foundation on Latimer's Brook and the brook itself, which runs alongside and under today's I-95 at its bend around the headwaters of the Niantic. Unlike the largely rural Lyme and the well-preserved Old Lyme to its west, the old Second Society of East Lyme has fully embraced the landscape-altering enterprises of the modern world, with all of the conveniences offered by corporate chain stores, providing the familiar comforts of a terrain that is recognizable and consistent in any town, anywhere in the United States and erasing that which made Flanders unique and quirky and provided the reason for the telling of this tale. Whether or not that is a mark of progress is up to the reader to decide. One can only speculate what Warren himself might make of the current state of his old stomping grounds.

In the end, perhaps the most recognizable surviving feature of Warren's world is the mill stream itself. In his diary entry of June 7, 1789, he writes that as a result of long drought "the loomy land is baked and cracked." No sooner had he made this entry in his diary than the rains came, heavier each day, with the downpour on June 10 being the "most extensive rainy day I ever knew." Four straight days of catastrophic flooding afflicted Flanders, with Latimer Brook breaking its banks and flooding over the tops of bridges at the mills, washing away the dams and finally the mills themselves. Water covered the road at Four Corners in front of Dr. Caulkins's home, and the raging floodwaters would force Warren and others to begin another summer rebuilding their enterprises from scratch.

Today, after big storms or especially rainy stretches, it's easy to see how Warren's world was rent asunder in 1789 by raging floodwaters, as the normally placid and easily ignored Latimer's Brook alongside I-95 becomes a raging whitewater rapid. Even with diversions and culverts, it's the one part of the landscape that resists taming. Today, with the help of fish ladders, alewives have returned to the mill stream. They had not been seen there since the dams were constructed over two hundred years ago. When stuck in traffic on a hot summer afternoon, one can look up and spy an osprey circling over the brook, tracking its meal, choosing the moment when it will fold its wings and dive into the water, snatching prey in talon and carrying it back to the nest. The osprey had nearly become extinct due to the effects of the Industrial Revolution Moses Warren helped initiate, but with conservation measures put in place a half century ago, the natural world is on the rebound, and despite the box stores and highway overpasses surrounding it, the site of Warren's millpond might even now be familiar to the old revolutionary trailblazer himself.

9

THE INSIDE-OUT PORCUPINE

An Algonquin legend says that deep in the mists of time, there was a porcupine who was unhappy with the form the Great Spirit had given it. This particular porcupine objected to having such a prickly exterior, which made it difficult to interact with other creatures. Time and time again, the porcupine pleaded with the Great Spirit to grant it a different form, until finally its wish was granted. As with many deeply desired wishes, this one was fulfilled in a way that was perhaps not what the wisher had envisioned. The Great Spirit decreed that since the porcupine wished to hide the beautiful quills it had been given, henceforth it would wear them on the inside, and changed it into the shad fish. This legend is the basis for the shad's nickname, "the inside-out porcupine," a reference to its numerous bones.

There are many other legends about the shad. Dutch and English settlers learned to fish for shad from Native Americans. The Dutch called it *elft* or "eleven fish," because it was supposedly the eleventh kind of fish they were able to identify in their new land. In the eighteenth century, shad was very popular, plentiful and very much in demand. Washington and Jefferson both wrote of their esteem for the sweet-tasting fish, and there are several accounts attesting that the early spring shad run up the Schuylkull River saved Washington's starving troops in 1778 after their harrowing winter at Valley Forge.

As an example of how plentiful shad once were in the Lymes, Wick Griswold notes in *Griswold Point* that Matthew Griswold IV, who was born

Shad fishing in the Connecticut River. *Old Lyme Historical Society Archive.*

at Black Hall in 1714, "built a series of docks and piers to accommodate his [shad] boats and nets. He rigged his dock with a large gun, which he fired off every time he landed a thousand shad. The gun was often heard several times a night."

In the eighteenth century, shad was eaten by rich and poor alike and was prized both for its seasonal abundance and inexpensive price. But by the mid-nineteenth century, attitudes grew somewhat stuffier and people became more concerned with "keeping up appearances." The newly minted middle classes especially worried whether they were wearing or doing or serving the correct thing. Because shad were so plentiful and inexpensive, they were deemed "common," and it was considered ungenteel to admit to eating them. Some shad aficionados went so far as to hide the pan they reserved for cooking shad. And it was never, ever to be served to guests. Still, the ever-practical people of the Lymes seem to have continued to relish their shad despite its distinct lack of gourmet cachet.

An 1844 fishing lease between Richard McCurdy of Old Lyme et al., as lessors, and a consortium of local fishermen as lessees, details the conditions by which the fishermen were allowed to use McCurdy's saltmarsh meadows and waterfront for fishing. The lease ran for twelve years, and during that time, the lessors agreed to pay "the value of one-fifteenth of all shad, bass, and salmon" taken at said fishery. The fishermen also agreed to "within a reasonable time, rebuild [the] pier, making it suitable and convenient for the hauling of seines," pay all taxes that might be assessed during the term of the lease, abide by the "proper season for taking fish," provide "suitable and sufficient seines, boats, and men" and give "proper attention to the business of fishing."

The rent was to be paid in money, but McCurdy and Co. also reserved the right to "call on the fishery and there receive the rent in fish" should they choose to do so. Another interesting detail of this lease is that at the end of the term, the lessees had the right to "remove and take away all the buildings, nets and capstans which they may have erected in the meadow."

A similar assemblage of buildings, capstans and nets used in combination with a stone pier was described in the *Bulletin of the Connecticut Historical Society*: "A small boat paid out a seine net on an incoming tide and then drew it back in a downriver sweep, making a loop and enclosing any fish that had run up against it. By 1818 more than eighty of these fish places lined the river as far north as Hartford."

Lyme had its full share of shad fishermen as well. Stanley Shuler's *Hamburg Cove* details the effort of local historians led by Elizabeth Plympton to collect and preserve papers and artifacts relating to shad fishing in Lyme, many of which are now in the collections of the Connecticut River Museum, the Mystic Seaport Museum and the Lyme Public Hall Association and Local History Archive (LPHA).

The LPHA also houses the Elizabeth Huey Putnam collection of papers and items regarding the Brockway's Ferry section of Lyme, including notes and artifacts from her father, Robert Huey, a noted stonemason and shad fisherman. Putnam wrote that her father was born in Donegal, Ireland, in 1868. He left school at seven years old to tend sheep and immigrated to America at age eighteen. Huey worked at quarries in Western Pennsylvania, where he learned the art of stonecutting. In 1888, he moved to Connecticut and worked at the Joshua's Rock quarry and Brockway's Ferry quarry. Huey was also a well-known shad fisherman for over fifty years. Putnam says, "One spring he registered two shad nets. At the time, he had two double-ended boats which he had built himself. Three of his grandsons, ages 16, 14, and 12 had commercial licenses to fish." In addition to selling locally, Huey and other Lyme shad fishermen shipped much of their catch to markets in Hartford and New York.

The American shad (*Alosa sapidissima*) is an anadromous fish. It is born in fresh water, lives most of its life in saltwater and returns to the freshwater place of its birth to spawn. In Connecticut, the shad run occurs in early

Lyme Shad fisherman Robert Huey with net. *Lyme Public Hall and Local History Archives.*

spring, and interested fisherfolk watch the landscape for hints that the shad are on their way. As spring arrives, the waters begin to warm up, and the forsythia and shadbush begin to blossom. These are traditional signs that the shad run is about to begin. Shad are the largest member of the herring family. They are silvery in color with a line of brownish speckles and a brown-green band on their backs. The U.S. Fish and Wildlife Service says a shad may swim up to twelve thousand miles in its lifetime, and a female shad can lay up to 600,000 eggs. In 2003, the shad was designated the Connecticut state fish by the general assembly.

Because of its numerous bones, shad must be filleted by an expert using special techniques, which can take years to perfect. These techniques were closely guarded and passed down along the generations. Many old-timers would quickly cover their work when someone walked into the room.

Old Lyme's Dawn Root is one of a very few experienced shad boners still practicing her craft today. In 2016, William Sisson interviewed her for *Angler's Journal*, in which Root said she'd learned how to bone shad as a young girl by watching her mother, Geri, and practicing with a butter knife. She described the process as having "24 cuts on each side of the fish, 48 total." The Root family owned Old Lyme Seafood, a fish market on the Black Hall River, which had been in business for fifty years before moving to New London in 2019. Dawn's father, Harry, was a fisherman who bought shad from local fishermen to augment his own catch. Though shad has become scarcer and less popular today, many people in Old Lyme will surely miss the days when Ms. Root's distinctive "Fresh Boned Shad" sign appeared outside her shop each spring.

Shad is often fished using a Brockway skiff, a flat-bottomed boat perfected by the late Richard "Earle" Brockway, of Old Saybrook. Brockway's design was very sturdy and almost extreme in its simplicity—crafted of construction-grade lumber and plywood. This style has become a nautical icon. The Sound School produced an instructional pamphlet that gives the history of the Brockway skiff and contains instructions for building one. Those interested in seeing a Brockway skiff in person should pay a visit the Shad Museum in Haddam. This small museum is only open on weekends during shad season, but it is filled with items relating to every aspect of shad and shad fishing and is located in a former "Shad Shack" at 212 Saybrook Road in the Higganum section of Haddam.

10

DAVID RUGGLES AND THE STRUGGLE FOR THE AMERICAN SOUL

Davide Ruggles, a native son of Lyme, is an American hero whose courage and sacrifice helped this nation on its journey to fulfill the promise of the ideals upon which it was founded. Like other Lyme heroes Samuel Holden Parsons, Stephen Johnson and Katharine Ludington, Ruggles is virtually unknown to the general public. Perhaps their relative anonymity is a result of Lyme's Yankee modesty or the lack of a Longfellow to memorialize its notable citizens. Or, perhaps, it is a function of the national memory that can only carry a few luminaries from the past into contemporary consciousness and requires a simple narrative to explain its history and understand its present. As a nation, we are disadvantaged by not being better acquainted with Mr. Ruggles, without whom another great figure in our history, Frederick Douglass, might have never risen to fame and inspired the citizenry to live up to a standard set by the founders, a standard that had not nearly been met, even by some of those founders—the genuine acceptance of the self-evident truth that all men are created equal and the duty of government to guarantee the opportunities of life, liberty and the pursuit of happiness for all citizens.

Born in Lyme in 1810, David Ruggles's parents, David Ruggles Sr. and Nancy Ruggles, were both free blacks living in a town that was in the final stages of abolishing slavery. Successful in their trades, David Sr. a blacksmith and Nancy a revered cook and caterer, the Ruggles soon moved from agrarian Lyme to the Bean Hill section of neighboring Norwich, a town quickly growing in economic stature and political influence. The Bean Hill neighborhood in which they settled provided a great deal of opportunity, both in terms of work and social connections. It was remarkably diverse—home to a vibrant community of free black merchants and craftspeople as well as some of the city's most prominent white families. The grand street around the green featured the mansions of Huntingtons, Clevelands and Hydes, while the more modest quarters located on back streets and alleys were the domain of a growing and respected black community. While it would be a stretch to say the neighborhood was "integrated," the cheek-by-jowl association of citizens of different races and economic class allowed for a social cohesion, where the children of white and black parents, both wealthy and working class, easily played together, even when the elders kept to their own sides of the invisible lines between cultures.

The young David Ruggles received an excellent public education. Along with studying Latin, arithmetic and other typical subjects of the day, he was taught by a woman who would become one of America's most celebrated poets—Lydia Huntley Sigourney. This was a time when the United States of America was beginning to define itself as a nation, with open questions of race, gender and class that had yet to be answered. Sigourney's poetic work was part of the dialogue, and though she preceded the Transcendentalists, whose monumental achievements created a truly modern national literature that rendered Sigourney's efforts wooden in style and uncomfortably racist in terminology to contemporary readers, as a schoolteacher, she taught integrated classrooms and was sympathetic to the African American community she came to know personally. She was, in fact, a fervent abolitionist and someone who argued passionately for respecting both the African American and Native American communities. Ruggles would take his experience growing up in Connecticut—the personal confidence afforded by a fine education and social graces and courage acquired through exposure to diverse elements of society—and use it to his best advantage when he moved to New York City at the age of seventeen.

David Ruggles quickly found success in New York. By the end of 1828, with barely a year in Manhattan under his belt, he was operating a successful grocery store at 1 Cortlandt Street. He carried all the essentials: coffee, tea, flour, butter, rum, gin, brandy, wine, cordials, porter and cider. He also carried "Porto Rico sugars." In a telling advertisement for his grocery that appeared in the August 2, 1828 issue of *Freedom Journal*, he noted, "The sugars above mentioned are fine sugars—they are manufactured by free people, not slaves." In this early advertised practice of what we now term

David Ruggles portrait, undated charcoal. *Amistad Research Center, Tulane University/ctfreedomtrail.org.*

"fair trade," Ruggles set the mark for what would become the driving purpose of his life—the abolition of slavery.

Ruggles soon squared his actions as a businessman with the growing progressive causes of the time. In 1831, he joined the temperance movement and no longer sold spirits in his establishment. Alcohol was seen as an oppressive force in society, particularly on the working class, who suffered by drinking inferior, unregulated products to excess, and by women and children, who suffered domestic violence and impoverishment as a result of alcohol abuse in the family. By the 1830s, advocates for social justice united under the banners of abolition of slavery, universal suffrage for women and temperance. In these early days of the movement, David Ruggles was one of the leading lights and most committed firebrands. At 36 Lispenard Street, he opened a rooming house and made it his life's work to assist runaway slaves from the South, harboring them in his home and arranging for safe passage to points north and east on the Underground Railroad.

The Underground Railroad was a series of clandestine safe houses where abolitionists would shelter runaway slaves and help them make their journey to Canada, where slavery had been abolished, or to ports such as New Bedford, which was ardently abolitionist and kept slave catchers at bay. While slavery was now illegal in the Northern states, slave catchers still prowled the streets in many places looking for runaways and seeking a bounty for returning human property to their masters below the Mason-Dixon Line. New York City was a place of refuge for slaves, with resources available and opportunities for anonymously blending in with the general population, but it was also a place that attracted slave catchers for the same reason, making a long stay in the growing metropolis exceedingly dangerous. As a conductor on the Underground Railroad, Ruggles provided slaves with food and shelter and made the arrangements for their passage either up the Hudson River to Canada or out on the Long Island Sound to points east.

The Connecticut River was another conduit running due north to Canada, and Ruggles's hometown of Lyme at the mouth of the river was an active center on the Underground Railroad. Several houses in today's Lyme, East Lyme and Old Lyme have been cited as stops on the Underground Railroad, though it's difficult to confirm these legends due to the clandestine nature of the activity at the time. The Steven Peck House in Old Lyme—on the corner of Ferry Road at 6 Lyme Street—is traditionally cited as one such house, with its secret stairs and rooms and proximity to both the river and Post Road making it easy to imagine it as the ideal venue for these noble efforts.

The Moses Noyes II house, also known as the Noyes-Beckwith house at 32 Lyme Street has long been documented as another stop on the Underground Railroad. The house is famously known as the residence of Supreme Court justice Morrison R. Waite, who entertained President Rutherford Hayes on summer breaks from their official duties. The architectural survey by the federal government's Works Progress Administration and Federal Writer's Project in the late 1930s notes that the attic bedrooms of the house were used to hide fugitive slaves, and the Historic American Buildings survey conducted in the late 1960s by the State of Connecticut in conjunction with the Library of Congress confirms the attic rooms of the Noyes-Beckwith house as an Underground Railroad site. The Connecticut Freedom Trail currently lists 32 Lyme Street as an Underground Railroad landmark but mistakenly refers to it as the "Stephen Peck House," which is not the 32 Lyme Street house but rather the one at 6 Lyme Street. The details being what they are, still, there is little doubt that the town of Lyme played a significant role in helping Southern slaves escape to safety.

It is estimated that Ruggles helped one thousand slaves to freedom. While each individual was equally important, none would be more famous or significant to the national dialogue than the famed orator Frederick Douglass. In a testament to the importance of David Ruggles, Douglass wrote in his autobiography of being a fugitive slave, recently arrived in New York City in "a distressed situation" and finding relief at "the humane hand of Mr David Ruggles, whose vigilance, kindness, and perseverance I can never forget. I am glad of an opportunity to express, as far as words can, the love and gratitude I bear him." He went on to say, "I have been in New York but a few days, when Mr. Ruggles sought me out and very kindly took me to his boardinghouse at the corner of Church and Lispenard Street," where he was "attending to a number of other fugitive slaves, devising ways and means for their successful escape, and though watched and hemmed in on almost every side, he seemed more than a match for his enemies."

Ruggles arranged for Douglass to go to New Bedford, where he could find work as a caulker on vessels of the large whaling fleet. As Douglass suggests, Ruggles had a great many enemies and was in constant peril. He was not a meek, behind-the-scenes figure but a very public firebrand, who shamed and exhorted his fellow citizens to join the just cause of abolition. On the first floor of his boardinghouse, he operated one of the nation's first black-owned bookstores, carrying abolitionist literature and publishing numerous pamphlets, including an influential periodical of his own, the *Mirror of Liberty*. His rhetoric was fiery. In the *National Anti-Slavery Standard* on August 19, 1841, he wrote, "Rise, brethren, rise! Strike for freedom or die slaves."

"In our cause, mere words are nothing—action is everything," he declares and stresses that "our cause demands of us union and agitation—agitation and action, from east to west, from north to south." He was also a firm believer in direct action—sitting in the "whites only" sections of trains and steamboats and pioneering the tactics of civil disobedience that would mark the civil rights movement more than one hundred years later, when Martin Luther King Jr. and Rosa Parks used these nonviolent tactics of direct action to challenge the unjust laws of a social order that perpetuated oppression based on race.

Pacifism, nonviolent resistance and civil disobedience have deep roots in the American political landscape. While King often cited Gandhi as an inspiration, and Gandhi cited Thoreau's essay on civil disobedience as an influence, it must be noted that Ruggles died in 1849, the year that Thoreau published his essay. Indeed, Ruggles's tactics were in harmony with those of abolitionist William Lloyd Garrison, and together they were early avatars of civil disobedience and passive resistance—strategies that embarrass authorities attempting to enforce unjust laws and deprive them of the excuse to employ violence as a means of enforcement, as violence is one of the few tools exclusive of the state and a mark of its authority. Given his proper place, Ruggles should be recognized by every American as one of the first heroes to help our nation in its struggle to ameliorate blights on the national character by overturning slavery and later the Jim Crow laws, which permitted legal discrimination and segregation until the Civil Rights Acts of 1964 and 1965 guaranteed voting rights and addressed the question of equal protection that had been promised in the U.S. Constitution.

Like most activists, Ruggles paid a high price for his efforts. His bookstore was burned down, but he quickly rebuilt. He suffered numerous assaults and twice escaped the attempts of kidnappers to capture him and bring him to the South to be sold into slavery. With his health in rapid decline, he left New York City and returned to his native New England, where he died at the untimely age of thirty-nine. He is buried at the Yantic Cemetery in Norwich, near Bean Hill, where he grew up. Though in the intervening years the cause for which he fought would tear the nation asunder time and again, with a horrific Civil War breaking out twelve years after his death, the justness of his words and deeds resonated in the actions of those fighting for justice over the course of the twentieth century. Even if his name has been nearly forgotten, his vigilance set the standard for which Americans could strive in their struggle to create a more perfect union and redeem the principles of liberty on which the nation was founded. And as a native of the land, David Ruggles must certainly be remembered and counted among Lyme's great luminaries.

II

Captain Sill's Midnight Escapes

Captain John Sill is a romantic figure in the history of Old Lyme. He was said to be an intelligent soul, a well-educated and rather dashing figure of good family, who took the beautiful and spirited Abigail Noyes for his wife. Despite this honorable background, Sill comes to us through history and legend as a smuggler—a customs runner of fine fabrics, who was arrested around 1820. His house on Lyme Street, designed by noted architect Samuel Belcher and crafted by shipwrights, with its secret closet that housed contraband silks, satins and laces, still stands.

The WPA Guide to Connecticut describes the Captain John Sill house as "a square yellow frame structure with white trim, its doorway now somewhat obscured by a later piazza. As originally designed by [Samuel] Belcher, a flight of steps led up to the door. The quoins at the corners and wide balustrade around the roof show what an effect of dignity and simplicity Belcher could achieve without the use of columns."

The book goes on to describe the secret "closet hidden within a cupboard" in which the captain hid his smuggled goods and related that Sill "was removed to New Haven and placed under bond not to leave that town. But according to tradition, Captain Sill often sped by night on horseback to Saybrook, thirty six miles distant, where a cousin rowed him across the river to his young wife who was waiting on the opposite shore."

The Society of Colonial Dames of America included the Sill House in its study of historic homes, *Old Houses of Connecticut*, stating, "The force of carpenters and joiners were ship and boat builders, for Lyme in those

John Sill house, Old Lyme, 2019. *James Meehan.*

days was something of a shipping point and on almost every section of the Lieutenant River, not cut off from the river channel by stretches of meadow, was located a shipyard. The oak timbers of the frame of this house and the beautifully fitted oak pins show that in those days workmen knew how to 'hew a line' and cut and fit and pin with a nicety that is unknown to the carpenter of the present commercial age."

After commending the workmanship of these nautically trained artisans, the Dames turned their attention to the famous hidden cupboard and related legend:

> *There is a closet under the eaves, in a storeroom in the second story of the North wing, said to be a smuggler's closet, where John Sill is supposed to*

have concealed rich silks, satins and laces. At any rate, he was arrested for smuggling and taken to New Haven where he was placed under bond not to leave the city limits. Here, whether guilty or not of evading the custom laws, he proved his devotion to his young wife. After dark on many a night, he would mount a swift horse—horses are always swift in a yarn of this kind—ride thirty six miles to the Saybrook Shore of the Connecticut, and there signal by lantern to Enoch Noyes, a cousin of his wife, who lived on the Lyme side of the river. Then would follow a ride in a silently rowed boat down the Connecticut [River] and up the Lieutenant River to the back door of John Sill's house, that he might have a short interview with his wife; then back by the same route to the Saybrook Shore where a fresh horse awaited him for the thirty six mile ride back. The rising sun would find him in New Haven as if nothing had happened.

Truly an astonishing tale—thirty-six miles each way and two rivers to navigate. Captain Sill and cousin Enoch must have been made of pretty sturdy stock, not to mention the fascinating Abigail, who inspired such a journey.

In 2018, the Old Lyme Historical Society was given a full set of very fine china embossed with the Sill family crest and motto. The pieces were found in a hidden cupboard in the attic by subsequent owners of the house, and it is believed that they date from Captain Sill's era.

Today, the Sill house is home to the Lyme Academy of Fine Arts, which was founded in 1976 by Elisabeth Gordon Chandler. The academy was later accredited as a college and renamed Lyme Academy College of Fine Arts. Chandler, who was arguably at least as interesting as Abigail Sill, started her career as a concert harpist and then became a professional sculptor and advocate for traditional representational art. From 2014 through 2019, the college was affiliated with the University of New Haven. Today, though it no longer has a degree program, Lyme Academy continues to offer student and adult classes and workshops in fine art.

12

I Hear the Train a Comin'

The lush verdure of Lyme summers—the thick rolling carpets of greens so deep they can seem blue-black—swept by salt breeze and bathed in the refracted light of garnet, quartz and moonstone from the shore, all this and more attracts the overheated denizens of New England and French Canada who come down the river valley to partake in the pleasures of the coast's high season. But Lyme's almost jungle-like summer foliage hides the secrets of its landscape from these fair-weather visitors: when the breezes turn chill and blow from the east, the leaves turn brilliant hues of crimson and gold and finally fall, leaving barren branches; then the snows leave a cover of white on the land—it is only then that the architecture of the landscape reveals itself. The ridges and hollows, the boulders and stone walls that wind through the woods and here and there strange constructions that could be one hundred or one thousand years old are suddenly evident in plain sight, inviting investigation.

Perhaps this is why Lyme Art Colony painter Henry C. White complained that the summer landscape in Lyme was just "too much spinach." The tonalist preferred the off-season, when the logic of the landscape revealed itself.

Driving along Shore Road in winter, heading east from the beaches of Old Lyme toward Niantic, one notices, just past Hatchett's Point Road and before the Amtrak train overpass, a massive granite wall in the woods on the south side of the road. It sticks out like the ruins of a castle wall—a dry stack of cut granite laid with expert precision and artistry, attracting the attention of the curious driver. The driver might also notice, on the other

Rock ledges and single-track railbed four miles east of the Connecticut River—site of 1864 accident with Civil War soldiers. *Jim Lampos.*

side of the street, two parallel stone walls about thirty feet apart, bordering what appears to be an old roadbed heading off into the woods and, even more strangely, a straight line of reeds bisecting a swamp just where the beach houses end and the woods begin. As they are in Old Lyme, one thing is clear: these stones and this slightly off-kilter landscape have a story to tell.

The tale involves ten Civil War soldiers who died at this very spot. It also involves tramps engaged in shootouts with conductors, and workers who got their heads blown off by dynamite. How can all this be, here in the rustic woods of Old Lyme? Let's take the story from the top.

What we're seeing in these strange constructions are the remains of the original single-track railroad built in 1851. Most of Amtrak's Northeast Corridor runs over the original track bed, which was elevated, straightened and double-tracked in the 1890s. The portion near Hatchett's Point, however, was abandoned when the tracks were relocated a few hundred feet north, with a new, deeper cut made through the bedrock ledge. While there were other abandoned stretches of track along the Northeast corridor, almost all have been repurposed by subsequent development. But in Old Lyme, things

Railbed at Hatchett's Point, 2019. *Jim Lampos.*

tend to linger longer than you'd expect, and the original single-track bed remains intact in the woods, inviting investigation.

Because of the forbidding geology of salt marshes and north–south oriented ribs of rock ledge, the railroad came through the Lymes fairly late. The brilliant civil engineer Alexander C. Twining was chosen to survey the route. The Yale-educated Twining was a multifaceted individual. He was a noted abolitionist who established one of Connecticut's first antislavery societies in 1825. He was a pioneer in the invention of refrigeration, developing the first vapor-compression system for the mechanical production of ice. He also designed the civic water system for the city of New London. But he is perhaps best known as the engineer who surveyed the routes for the railroad throughout Connecticut, Vermont, upstate New York and the Great Lakes and drew up plans for their construction.

The first passenger train was introduced in England in 1825. One year later, trains made their debut in the United States, with a three-mile line built from Quincy, Massachusetts, to Bunker Hill to carry granite for the construction of the monument there. The first reliable steam locomotive, Tom Thumb, was developed by famed inventor, philanthropist, educator and abolitionist Peter Cooper in 1830, inaugurating the age of the train. Journalists breathlessly promoted this new transportation technology. An editorial in the *Connecticut Journal* on January 26, 1830, stated, "Gentlemen will keep their own steam coaches. Stables will cease to be an annoyance; steam carriages will be patient animals, never kicking for flies, nor whisking their tails in men's mouth, nor sending out horsesome odors."

Inventors like Twining and Cooper were born into a world where travel across land could only be accomplished by one of two means—by foot or by horse. Travel by sea was easier in some ways, but this, too, relied on the brawny strength of a rower or the vicissitudes of Mother Nature and her variable winds to fill canvas sails and propel seagoing vessels. A journey from Boston to New York was filled with uncertainty. A packet sloop could take anywhere from three to nine days to go from New York City, up the Long Island Sound and into the port of Providence, where the journey would be completed overland to Boston.

Attempts to provide regular, reliable transportation were made early in Connecticut. In 1717, the general assembly authorized Captain John Munson to "set up a wagon to pass and transport passengers and goods between Hartford and New Haven." Thus public transportation was born in the colony, and part of Munson's exclusive license deal from the government obligated him to maintain a regular schedule—departing the first Monday of the month and returning that week, weather permitting. By 1789, stagecoaches had become a common means of transit. The four- to six-day journey between Boston and New York was handled by a total of two coaches and twelve horses. At full capacity, the stagecoaches carried fewer than two thousand passengers a year, indicating the relative rarity of overland travel in New England in that era.

In 1792, the turnpike era dawned in New England, with the creation of the Mohegan Road between Norwich and New London—the region's first toll road. The Mohegan Road was actually an ancient Indian footpath, improved by Joshua Raymond into a primary road in 1670 and finally leveled, straightened and widened in the early 1790s, with tolls erected to help pay for improvements and maintenance. Over the next half century, more than 120 corporations were franchised to create fee-based turnpikes across Connecticut, many of which survive today, though the tollhouses are long gone. The Boston Post Road, or Route 1 through the Lymes, which had been known as the "country road," was transformed into the Lyme New London Turnpike in 1807, facilitating transportation between the Thames and Connecticut Rivers and replacing the old Post Road along today's Route 156 as the primary route through this part of the state.

The early nineteenth century also saw the development of the steamboat. Robert Fulton's *Cleremont* was introduced in 1807 for service on the Hudson River, and by 1815, steamships started appearing in Connecticut ports. Captain Stevens Rogers of New London commanded the *Savannah*, the first steamship to cross the Atlantic in 1819, though it would be decades before steamships replaced sailing vessels on the ocean crossing. Regular service between New London and New York City began in 1816 and took twenty-one hours to complete, saving considerable time.

The Lymes joined the age of steam in 1824, with the introduction of regular steamship service on the Connecticut River with connections to Hartford, Sag Harbor and New York City. Stagecoaches met the steamships at the terminus of the Lyme Turnpike at Calves Island on the Connecticut River near today's Old Lyme Marina. In the 1850s, several steamships stopped at Lyme. The *Island Belle* provided direct service to Sag Harbor. Leaving Lyme at 1:00 p.m., it would arrive in Greenport, Long Island, at 2:45 p.m. and at the commercial hub that was the whaling port of Sag Harbor at 3:30 p.m. The *Cricket* also made connections to Orient Point, Greenport and Sag Harbor via New London. The fare to New London from Lyme was fifty cents, and it cost a dollar to get to Sag Harbor. Going north from Lyme, the *Cricket* zig-zagged up the Connecticut River, with stops at Ely's

Ice sailing at Ely's Ferry circa 1900. *Lyme Public Hall and Local History Archives.*

Ferry, Deep River, Chester, Hadlyme, Goodspeed, Keeney's Landing, Red Store, Rock Landing, Higganum, Middle Haddam, Middletown, Rocky Hill and Hartford. The forty-five-mile sail from Lyme to Hartford took five hours. Service on these steamship lines was seasonal, with ice choking the Connecticut River in winter.

The winter of 1856 was particularly harsh. The *Hartford Courant* reported that one could still cross the Connecticut River on the ice as late as April 1 that year. Mr. E.L. Brockway of Saybrook crossed from Saybrook to Lyme twice each day on April 1 and 2 in 1856, with the ice thick enough to support his horse and sleigh. On April 1, William C. Spencer crossed from Hadlyme to Chester with a horse and sleigh at full speed and loaded with a company of ladies and gentlemen. In a typical year, the river would be clear of ice by April, and steamships would begin their runs early in the month. In 1853, for example, the *Island Belle* began her runs on April 5.

But the days of the turnpike and steamship were numbered. The railroad would change everything. Journeys that took days could now be done in hours, and those that took hours would be measured in minutes. Neither rain nor sleet nor excessive heat or cold affected the railroad, and service continued even in the snow. Alexander Twining had been surveying and drawing construction plans for railroads all over the country since the 1830s. But the stretch from New Haven to New London through the Lymes proved particularly vexatious. The numerous inlets and marshes and the rugged bedrock ridges that ribbed the landscape made an east–west route along the shore difficult for the railroad. Finally, in 1849, Twining set to work to survey the route from New Haven to New London.

In his 1836 survey for the New Haven and Hartford Railroad, Twining noted that "a trap ledge…will create the expense of considerable excavation through rock." The steepest inclinations a train could handle at the time were thirty feet per mile. Through the Lymes, Twining would have to choose a route that clung close to the shore, avoiding the excessive blasting through ledge that he would have to do if he went even a mile or two inland. While the use of gunpowder to split rock had been known in the region since 1759, when the technique was used in the construction of one of New London's Hempstead Houses, it remained an expensive and dangerous proposition through the mid-nineteenth century. On September 26, 1851, during construction of the New Haven and New London Railroad, James Pickett was killed by an accidental discharge while blasting ledge. The *Courant* reported that the "Blast didn't explode so he renewed it with powder, and was in the act of ramming it down with a stick when it suddenly exploded, blowing his head to atoms."

Construction of the New Haven and New London Railroad through the Lymes was an incredibly labor-intensive task, with most of the work done by hand, horse and oxen. On March 11, 1851, 2,000 men were working on building the railroad. By October 18, that number had more than doubled to 4,500. Before construction, the fifty-two-mile rail line was estimated by Twining to cost $1,414,350. After completion of construction, the final audit showed an actual cost of $1,456,319, proving his estimate remarkably accurate.

The quality of Twining's work is evident today if you're walking the abandoned stretch of track near Hatchett's Point. He specified that his single-track roadbed should be thirty feet wide at grade level, with all masonry being "dry work" and bridges being "simple truss work" sustained by abutments. Dry work refers to an ancient technique of stone construction using no mortar but only the form and weight of the rocks themselves to provide stability and strength. The entire enterprise relied on the skill of the stonemason. The quality of work is evidenced by the bridge abutment that still stands just south of Shore Road at Hatchett's Point. Not a stone is out of place. It bore the weight of Shore Road traffic for more than one hundred years and continues to stand undiminished today.

The railroad bed itself is remarkably level, given that it is nearly 170 years old and has been abandoned for 130 years. To prevent frost heaves, Twining recommended that the bed be constructed of stone slabs twenty inches square and three and a half to four inches thick and embedded in sand. Earth and gravel were then laid over the slabs and red cedar "transverse sleepers" with a cast-iron chair screwed into them, thus completing the railbed. While the rails are now gone, the 1851 workmanship remains intact on the landscape—a testament to the expertise of surveyor and mason alike.

After a year and a half of construction, the New Haven and New London Railroad opened on July 6, 1852, with trains reaching the Connecticut River. By July 22, trains were running from Lyme to Brown's Wharf in New London. While service began with only one train running from New Haven on July 6, by August 20, three trains made the daily trip from New Haven to New London, and the terminus in New London shifted to Lawrence Wharf. By November of that year, the New London depot was built.

In the first nine months of operation, the railroad carried 101,640 passengers from New Haven to New London. An "old timer" quoted in the *New Haven Register* on May 11, 1931, recalled that "it took 3 hours to make the trip and people thought they were going like lightning." Indeed, by the standard of the day, they were. A trip that once would have taken a full day in good conditions could now be completed between breakfast and lunch. By 1854, travel time had improved to such a degree that it nearly matched today's pace. A train leaving New Haven at 7:45 a.m. would arrive in Lyme by 9:30 a.m. and East Lyme at 9:54 a.m. The journey from Lyme to New York City, which would have taken several days only ten years before, could now be accomplished in four and a half hours.

The earliest trains on the line were built by the Rogers, Ketchum and Grosvenor Company in Paterson, New Jersey—later the Rogers Locomotive and Machine Works, the leading train manufacturer of the day. With their big balloon stacks, these trains burned wood to heat the water in the boiler and create steam. Wood was 14 percent of the total operating cost, with the greatest single cost being labor at 22 percent.

Unforeseen repairs took their toll. A steamboat ferrying trains over the Connecticut River had to be taken out of service when its boilers were damaged due to the use of the river's saltwater for cooling. The New Haven and New London annual report of 1854 stated that the damage "required a considerable sum for repairs, and arrangements have been made for supplying the boilers with fresh water." Still, with dedicated local men, such as Lyme's Daniel Chadwick, serving on its board, the railroad managed to turn a modest profit that year, showing an income of $96,137.00 against operating expenses of $96,054.00. The ride from New Haven to Lyme

New Haven, New London and Shoreline Railroad, 1860. *David Peters Collection, Archives and Special Collections at the Thomas J. Dodd Research Center, UCONN Library.*

cost $0.95, with $0.10 charged per station heading east. For example, New Haven to Black Hall, Lyme's second station, was $1.05, and it was $1.15 to South Lyme, the third station. Three daily trains carried a total of 164,754 passengers that year with no injuries.

The railroad cracked Lyme open. As an 1876 *Harper's Weekly* article noted, the town had always prided itself on its "moral and intellectual character" and "self respecting inner life," but the early nineteenth century had not been kind. Lyme suffered a decades-long decline in its economy and population. Farmers moved to more fertile fields in the Western Reserve of Ohio and later moved on to the Midwest or followed the gold rush to California. Some went to sea to hunt the whale. The shipbuilding industry moved to deeper harbors, and the small mills along laconic streams could no longer compete with the larger enterprises flourishing in towns such as Worcester, Lowell, Waterbury and Norwich. The Industrial Age left Lyme behind.

Citing its reputation for having a salubrious atmosphere, upright citizenry and a centuries-long tradition of quality public education, "friends of the New Haven and New London Rail Road," such as James Brewster Esq., wrote letters to the editor promoting Lyme as a refuge for parents seeking the ideal place to raise their children: "If the city is the right place to make money, it is the wrong place to bring up children. The prosperous men in the city were reared in the country. It is rare to see a prosperous, intelligent, moral man in the cities of Boston and New York who were educated there. They commit a great mistake who go to New York to bring up children. They may accumulate wealth, and their children die in the almshouse. There is DEATH there."

An 1857 piece in the *Hartford Courant* used Lyme's reputation for fine schools and recreational attractions as a drawing card to lure wealthy families: "Till within a few years, Lyme seemed almost closed to the traveler. But railroads and boats now made it of easy access. Its union of inland and sea-side pleasures will make it, more and more, the resort of the more sober class, who leave the city for a house in the country during the warm season."

It goes on to say, "It has long been known that Lyme has its educated and cultivated circle. If parents wish to place their sons in a private or select school they will find one of the first order."

One hundred years before people across America fled the crowded inner cities for the promise of idyllic life in the suburbs, Lyme was already enticing the family squire to leave the metropolis and raise his progeny in the paradise of the countryside, all within easy commuting distance on the steamboat or locomotive to his affairs in the capitals of commerce. Over the next century, Lyme would become a summer resort that attracted the likes of Woodrow Wilson, Felix Frankfurter and Albert Einstein. It would also host artists from New York City, such as Henry Ward Ranger and Childe Hassam, who would help found the Lyme Art Colony and make Old Lyme the home of American Impressionism.

But while Lyme was beginning this transformation with the introduction of the railroad in 1852, the nation itself was about to plunge into a horrific battle that pitted state against state, North against South and abolitionist against slaveholder. The brutality of war that would break out, with its stunning slaughter on the battlefields of Pennsylvania, Virginia, the Carolinas and Georgia, would tear the nation's soul asunder. It would touch every aspect of every citizen's life. Men from Lyme, where abolition had been a strong sentiment for more than half a century, volunteered for the Union cause, and many died on the battlefields of the South. Lyme native Robert McCurdy, now a successful businessman in New York City, was among the first to raise money in support of the United States Army. And while no battles were fought on Lyme soil, at least ten Civil War soldiers were killed in Old Lyme in October 16, 1864, at the very spot where the massive stonework of the abandoned original single-track rail stands near Hatchett's Point.

It was a Saturday afternoon. Six passenger cars were carrying 275 sick and wounded soldiers from Knight's Hospital in New Haven to Readville, Massachusetts, where they would receive further care. As the train followed the shoreline route through Old Lyme, it passed "through a deep cut of rocks about four miles east of the Connecticut River, known as Rocky Ledge." While later reports corrupted the name to "Rocky Neck," all reports placed the location four miles east of the river. The initial *Hartford Courant* report of October 17 had it right—it was Rocky Ledge. Four miles east of the Connecticut River places us right at the site of the large stonework that's visible in the woods just south of Shore Road near Hatchett's Point Road. A walk down the old railbed shows a high rock ledge rising on both sides to a height of approximately twenty feet. The ledge shows telltale signs of blast holes. And the dry stack stone construction was the abutment for the Shore Road bridge that passed overhead. This narrow channel with high rock ledges on both sides was absolutely the worst place for a six-car train, each car crammed with 45 sick and wounded soldiers returning from the battlefield, to derail.

The train was tossed from the track by a broken rail. The *Courant* reported, "The cars were dashed against the solid rock on either side, and one of them, in the middle of the train, was thrown up and across the track, forming a complete arch some 20 feet above the road. In the clash of iron and stone, ten soldiers and two railroad workers were instantly killed. A dozen more were seriously wounded, and an additional 25 were injured."

Among the dead were L.V. Philips of the Thirty-Second Massachusetts, Edward Dalton of the Tenth New Hampshire, George Dynes of the Twenty-Fifth Massachusetts, William Maffit of the Sixth Connecticut, Montgomery Cosen of the Sixth Connecticut, Alexander McGregor of the First Massachusetts, Thomas Johnson of the Fifty-Ninth Massachusetts, Richard A. Young of the V.R. Corps, Richard Baxter of Massachusetts and N.W. Doyle of Chestnut Street Hospital in Philadelphia, along with railroad brakemen Edgar Parsons of Berlin, Connecticut, and Horace Beebee of New London.

The dead and wounded were returned to Knight's Hospital in New Haven, and the remaining survivors were forwarded to their destinations via the Hartford route to Boston. Superintendent Calhoun ordered the damaged cars burned, and by the next evening, regular rail service had resumed.

We will never know if this was an accident or an act of sabotage. Foul play on the rail line was not unheard of. A report from August 17, 1868, states, "a dastardly attempt was made to throw the express train on the Shore Line Railroad which leaves New London at 2:30 off the track at Stoney Creek." The train had first experienced trouble at Lyme Station, when a coupling between the baggage and passenger cars broke. But at Stoney Creek, the train encountered a rail placed diagonally across the track and another, three hundred feet farther along, deliberately laid to derail the train. This was not just kids placing rocks or pennies on the tracks. In this incident, there were injuries but no fatalities.

The stonework and ledge at the abandoned single-track line near Hatchett's Point stand as a silent memorial to these Civil War dead who died tragically, far from the battlefield. Covered by the lush canopy of maples and oaks in summer, it is only in winter that these granite memorials reveal themselves. The success of the railroad through the late nineteenth century prompted the realignment, straightening, elevation and double-tracking of the line in 1890, leaving this short stretch of single track to revert back to nature in this bucolic corner of Old Lyme. The double-tracking was necessitated by the completion of the train bridge over the Thames River. The three daily trains of 1852 had increased to ten by 1869, and by the turn of the century, more than thirty daily trains plied the route that is today's Northeast Corridor.

The expansion of train service also brought some unwanted visitors. On May 15, 1896, a gunfight between the train conductor and some tramps broke out at the South Lyme station. The *Hartford Courant* article from that day states, "This section has been overrun with tramps. Five tramps controlled extra freight train No. 285 from New London to this place tonight and leaving the train have exchanged shots with the conductors."

Sound View Station, March 19, 1930. *David Peters Collection, Archives and Special Collections at the Thomas J. Dodd Research Center, UCONN Library.*

Sound View Depot, Shore Line Railroad. *David Peters Collection, Archives and Special Collections at the Thomas J. Dodd Research Center, UCONN Library.*

A report from later that summer indicates the problem was widespread: "Large numbers of tramps frequent the beach begging food, probably on the way from New Haven to New London or vice versa." It goes on to say that the problem is "not new by any means."

As early as 1867, the Connecticut legislature felt compelled to introduce an act discouraging layabouts, hobos and tramps: "No adult person shall cling to or jump upon any locomotive or train car except in compliance with the rules of the company; also that persons shall not lounge about rail depots," noting that there has been a "great inconvenience caused to passengers at many stations by persons lounging about the depots."

The influx of "undesirables" on the rail line was actually an indicator of its success. At the beginning of the twentieth century, the railroad through Old Lyme and East Lyme was an embedded institution that spurred development and, in turn, prospered as a result of the influx of new residents, summer visitors and tourists. Old Lyme had been served by two stations in the beginning: Lyme Station at the Connecticut River and South Lyme. The Black Hall Station was soon added, and in 1902, a whistle-stop was established at Sound View with a passenger shelter. Sound View grew so rapidly, in large part due to the train service, that the Black Hall Station was relegated to a freight siding, and Sound View received a new full-service station in 1906. In East Lyme, stations were established at Crescent Beach and Niantic, serving the hordes of fair-weather visitors, including the devotees of the Spiritualist Camp at Pine Grove. The Spiritualists may have been entertained by the short-lived "Ghost Train," an all-white train with gold trim and a crew dressed in white that ran at night along the shoreline to great dramatic effect.

Rapid developments in technology improved speed, reliability and comfort. Enclosed cars, introduced by 1860, were quickly followed by parlor and smoking cars. Coal replaced wood as a reliable fuel source, and by the twentieth century, the larger, more powerful engines were fueled by diesel. Electrification of the line was proposed as early as 1912, and the first electrified portion was opened in 1919. While the whole corridor along the Connecticut coast was slated for electrification from the beginning, it was not actually completed until 1996.

The Northeast Corridor remains the most heavily traveled and profitable segment of today's Amtrak system, but the railroad has suffered a steady decline from its nineteenth- and early-twentieth-century heyday, due to the one invention that utterly transformed the national landscape: the automobile. By the 1940s, all of the stations in Old Lyme and East Lyme had been taken out of service, with trains stopping only in Old Saybrook and New London. In Niantic, the railroad station was sold for $15,000 in 1949. It had fallen into disrepair and was in poor condition.

Lyme Station, March 19, 1930. *David Peters Collection, Archives and Special Collections at the Thomas J. Dodd Research Center, UCONN Library.*

In a natural passing of the transportation torch, the station was sold to Callahan Oil Company, which provided "White Flash Gasoline" to automobile drivers speeding along the newly made Blue Star Highway. Forgetting about the iron rails while measuring the potency of their machines in horsepower, they were getting ever further away from the world of their forefathers.

13

I Am Not Extinct

The Nehantics

A fault runs through our land. It begins in Lyme on the northern edge of Joshuatown, named for "Joshua the Indian," also known as Attawanhood, sachem of the Nehantics. It arcs easterly to the land of his father, Uncas, the seventeenth-century chief of the Mohegans and ally of the English, and directly under that tribal nation's current enterprise, the Mohegan Sun Casino, on the banks of the Thames River at Trading Cove. The fault travels east again to the sovereign land of the Pequots at the headwaters of the Mystic River near that tribal nation's gaming enterprise, Foxwoods Casino, and on to the foot of the highest summit in this region, Lantern Hill. This is the Honey Hill Fault, where worlds collide—where the primordial continents of Gander and Avalonia met proto–North America to create the ancient supercontinent Pangea and split apart again, leaving just a little piece of themselves behind.

The fault has been quiet lately, only emitting an occasional rumble now and then, but in the earliest days of English immigration to these Algonquin lands, it was active enough for John Winthrop Jr. to make note of its humbling power. He wrote that on June 1, 1638, "between 3 and 4 in the afternoon there was a great earthquake." "It came with a noise like a continual thunder or the rattling of coaches in London." It was powerful enough that "it shook ships that rode in the harbor."

Earthquakes regularly struck throughout the eighteenth century and were strong enough to knock chimneys down. Near the western end of the fault, the caves of Mount Tom just north of Lyme's border in Moodus, would sound with strange noises, explosions, cracks and groans. The Nehantics called this place Matchimoodus, or the "place of bad noises." In Mohegan, *matchi mundi* means "devil" or "demon." While the earthquakes have diminished in frequency and severity over the centuries, strange noises still emanate from Moodus, but that's another story.

In the Lymes, wherever you see a ridge leading to the sea, you're looking at the bones of the land itself. This is bedrock—gneiss—formed nearly a billion years ago and pushed up into ridges and valleys when the continent of Gander was caught in the middle of a collision between North America, west Africa and northern Europe. Joshua's Rock, near Eight Mile Island at the bend of the Connecticut River—is an exposed piece of towering bedrock that has long been a lookout spot and landmark for anyone surveying or navigating the great river and surrounding terrain. Unique in this region, Joshua's Rock is characterized by a heavy concentration of aegirine-augite, a lustrous black mineral rarely found in the United States and more frequently occurring along the Atlantic shores of Canada, Greenland, Norway and Scotland, as well as the coast of west Africa. Mystics dealing in crystal magic will tell you it's associated with change and transformation. Certainly,

Joshua's Rock, 2019. *Michaelle Pearson.*

Attawanhood, or Joshua the Indian to the English, stood on the precipice of profound change and transformation for his people.

Attawanhood's will, drafted in 1675, expressed his desire to have his children "be kept to the English school" and that he himself be buried "in a coffin after an English manner." Perhaps he clearly saw the material advantage the English would have over his people in the coming age. His father, Uncas, had been a loyal friend to the English and had assisted them in their conquest of the Pequots in a bloody battle on the hills of Mystic in 1637. The Pequot War, which occurred a mere two years after the English settlement of Connecticut coast, settled a simmering dispute between the newly arrived English immigrants and the natives of this land, as well as one between the Mohegan Sachem Uncas and his father-in-law, the Pequot Sachem Sassacus. Prior to the arrival of the English, Uncas became the leader of a renegade band of Pequots and settled his followers on the western shore of the Thames River in a place now called Uncasville, midway between Norwich and New London. With the Pequot defeat in 1637, all of the land in the Lymes fell under the domain of two parties—the Mohegans and the English.

The native tribe of the Lymes, however, was the Nehantics. They preceded both the Mohegans and Pequots and dwelled along the entire coast of eastern Connecticut and western Rhode Island. Native legend has it that the conquering Pequots came to southeastern Connecticut from the upper Hudson valley in the 1500s, and in making their stronghold the mouth of the Thames River, they split the Nehantic tribe in two, thus a reference to the western Nehantics and eastern Nehantics that persists to this day. The eastern Nehantics occupied the coast around Pawcatuck between the domain of the Pequots and Narragansetts, and the western part of the tribe occupied Lyme and Saybrook. In his seminal work, *The History of the Indians of Connecticut*, John William De Forest wrote, "The Pequots had conquered this portion of the Connecticut valley; and had obliged its original owners to submit to their authority."

In both legend and written history, the Nehantics have been characterized as the "peaceful," "quiet" or "gentle" tribe, wary of armed conflict or warfare. The Mohegans characterized the Nehantics as having high and soft-speaking voices. It was said from the earliest times that no Nehantic had ever killed an Englishman. The English at the time seem to have agreed, as they did not seek retribution against the Nehantics for the murder of Captain Stone, who was variously characterized as an innocent English trader or dissolute pirate slaver, in 1633. Even as that murder in Nehantic country precipitated an escalation of tensions between the native tribes and the English, with tit-for-tat retributions that finally led to all-out war in 1637, it was the Pequots the English fought not the Nehantics. Likewise, when Captain John Mason's band of soldiers scoured the coast between New London and Saybrook in search of hostile natives in the aftermath of the battle at Pequot Fort in Mystic, they fell on three hundred Nehantics who were accused of hiding Pequot warriors. The Nehantics made it clear that they wanted no part of the hostilities, saying they "wouldn't fight with English men, for they were Spirits." Unlike their Mohegan and Narragansett neighbors, they did not join the English in their battle against the Pequots, nor did they come to the Pequots' defense.

Nehantic histories and folk tales often speak to the humor and trickster spirit of their people as a means of survival. Mercy Nonesuch recounted her people's response to a siege by the Mohawks, who raided the Connecticut River valley with some frequency and were feared. She told Frank Speck, the early twentieth century's leading scholar on the native people of Connecticut, that on one occasion, a Mohawk raiding party had suddenly appeared in the land of the Nehantic without warning. With no time to muster a defense, the Nehantics hid in a set of caves called the Devil's Den at the headwaters of the Niantic River. They had no provisions, but quickly gathered and brought their mortars and pestles. The Mohawks stood guard by the cave entrance, planning to starve out the Nehantics, but when they heard joyful singing and the pounding of pestle on mortar coming from the caves, they were fooled into thinking that the empty-handed Nehantics were well provisioned and fortified for a long siege. The Mohawks, discouraged, gave up and left.

The Nehantics were best known for their handicrafts, from beadwork to basket making, and for the ample bounty of their land. Their best defense, it appears, was in accommodating those who wished to rule the coast by sharing their bounty or providing useful labor. In a beautifully poetic passage, a memorial from the Nehantics and Mohegans to the Connecticut General Assembly in 1784 states, "Supreme spirit above, made the great world.... The land was stored with all manner of four footed creatures both great and small, and the air was filled with variety of fowl of all sizes and colors, and our wild land was heavily loaded with all manner of wild fruit, and our seas, ponds, or lakes, rivers, and brooks were brimful of all sorts of fish of all bigness, even our sand and mud were well stored with shellfish."

It was, in their words, a "rich and well furnished world." The land's plenty is illustrated in a *New London Gazette* article from 1811, which reports that on

Mercy Nonesuch Matthews. *National Anthropological Archives, Smithsonian Institution.*

the night of January 5, four men caught 9,900 pounds of bass with a seine at the Niantic River headwaters and sold the catch in New York City for $300. This land was bountiful, and the Nehantics were giving and willing to share with the English.

Colonial authorities note a September 10, 1675 testimonial from Lyme's founder Matthew Griswold: "Upon a letter from the Niantick Indians, from Mr. Griswold, certifying their fidelity and good affection to the English, and some service done by them, the Councill sent a letter to them to assure them of our friendship, and that we should show them all suitable respect when there is occasion."

Even as the tribal members, struggling to survive as farmers, were abandoning their ancestral homes and setting off for the west or signing on to whaling ships at the end of the eighteenth century, they said of the immigrants to their land, "We immediately entered into strong friendship… having lived together like brothers almost two hundred years."

Despite this spirit of peace and cooperation the Nehantics extended to the English, the English did not treat them as equal sovereigns of the land but instead, sometimes inadvertently and sometimes deliberately, conducted a soft war of attrition against them over a period of 250 years—from the time they made first contact to the time they declared them extinct.

When the English arrived, the whole of the Lymes was Nehantic land. Peter Comstock, the Nehantic overseer, wrote in 1833 that "their title is from the supreme being and not written deeds" and "all the tribe lands belong equally to every individual of whatever sex or age." From the founding of Saybrook Colony in 1634, the English set about acquiring Nehantic land through both deed and conquest. Like all Native American communities in New England, the Nehantic population had been decimated through disease and contagion in the century between first European contact in the early sixteenth century and the founding of the English colonies in the early seventeenth. An estimated precontact population of four thousand had fallen to four hundred by the time of English settlement. The Nehantics must have believed that there was room for everyone in the bountiful land, and they were willing to share. It came as a shock to them, however, that when they were deeding land to the English and allowing them to dwell and raise crops there, the English expected exclusive rights and set about curtailing Nehantic hunting rights. To the Nehantics, this was inconceivable. Wildlife did not recognize the mapped and deeded boundaries of humans, and to survive, humans had to follow the wildlife regardless of whose property they "trespassed" on.

In the 1784 memorial, the Nehantics stated that though they sold the land, "hunting, fishing, and fowling we never have alienated—it is our birthright and that is now all gone." Even fishing in the Connecticut River, a privilege anyone can enjoy today, was denied to Nehantics by the English: "some white people have presumed to forbid us of fishing in certain places, especially in the Connecticut River....We think it is unnatural for rational creatures to forbid one another of that privilege."

The attempts by the English to circumscribe Nehantic rights began at the very foundation of the colony. The English immediately divided the Lymes and Nehantic lands following the Pequot War. The English laid claim to these lands by right of conquest, as the Pequots were the nominal rulers of Nehantic lands, though the Nehantics maintained their own communities, sachems and unique cultural attributes. But with the defeat of the Pequots, the English considered the Lymes to be theirs, save and except for the lands they recognized as being the domain of Uncas, their Mohegan ally.

John Winthrop the Younger, governor of Saybrook Colony and founder of the Pequot Plantation at New London, objected to this arrangement. In 1647, Winthrop petitioned the court, claiming he personally held title to "the whole country of the western Nehanticks, including a considerable part of the town of Lyme," which he had obtained "partly by purchase, partly by deed of gift." Winthrop produced three Nehantics and an interpreter, Thomas Stanton, as witnesses on his behalf, backing his claim that Chief Sashions of the Nehantics had deeded the Lymes to him in exchange for coats and other considerations. But as he could not produce a certified legal document as proof and did not press his claim before the Pequot War, the Connecticut commissioners denied Winthrop's claim and instead upheld the ownership of Lyme by the patentees and freemen of Saybrook Colony.

Thus Winthrop's domain extended only to the east bank of the Niantic River, and the Lymes were divided between English lands and Uncas's lands. To Uncas went the area of Lyme from the Connecticut River at Eight Mile Island, easterly through today's Salem and Montville to his fort at Shantok on the banks of the Thames. His third son, Attawanhood, whom the English called Joshua, was given control of the western portion of this tract from Eight Mile Island and inland along the north banks of the Eight Mile River—an area that came to be known as Joshuatown. He was also appointed sachem of the Nehantics. Also recognized as Indian land, though not always legally recorded as such, was the section of today's East Lyme that is known as Niantic. Niantic stretched from the shores of the bay of the same name, on the coast of Long Island Sound at Black Point and uplands to the north of the river and sound—a place called Indian Woods, where the coastal tribe kept their winter lodging.

Uncas had been acting as the leader of the Nehantics since the conclusion of the Pequot War. In 1658, when the Narrangansetts laid siege to his stronghold at Mohegan and forced him out of Fort Shantok, Uncas sought refuge in Nehantic territory and made his fort at the headwaters of the Niantic River. He was officially recognized as the Nehantic sachem in a 1666 treaty with Arramamet of the Podunks: "Uncas, sache of Moheag, on behalf of himself and people of Moheag and Nehantick" promises that they will conduct themselves "peaceably and neighborly toward them." Uncas, in turn, appointed Attawanhood as chief of the Nehantics. In 1672, Attawanhood married Arramamet's daughter Sowgonosh and inherited control of considerable Podunk holdings up the Connecticut River Valley in and around Hartford, making him a powerful player in Connecticut politics.

The Nehantics were not pleased with the appointment of Attawanhood as their leader. In his *Itineraries*, Ezra Stiles notes that there were essentially two chiefdoms among the Nehantics—one centered at Joshuastown and one in Niantic. The Niantic sachems, "Ould Sanup," "Ould Haguin" and

"Woompany," functioned more as respected tribal elders than as strong political leaders. They signed a protest against Attawanhood's elevation to Nehantick sachem, stating that "they were not willing to take Joshua," as he would bring them trouble. Sanup petitioned John Winthrop in 1668, asking permission for the Nehantics to live by themselves and not under the rule of Attawanhood. The reputation of Uncas and his sons as warlords, battling both the Pequots and Narragansetts, did not sit well with the peaceful Nehantics. Still, it is the strong arm that stretches the bow, and the gentle tribe had no choice but to assent.

Also in 1672, a three-hundred-acre Nehantic reservation was created at Black Point. Though they had gained legal title to this portion of their ancestral lands, the Nehantics, in effect, lost the right to enjoy the bounty of their traditional world that extended beyond this modest coastal reservation. They didn't gain a reservation; they lost a birthright. While some tribal members owned parcels outside of the reservation, the Nehantics were no longer free to roam their traditional hunting grounds, and their world became circumscribed. Even this diminished world, comprising Joshuastown in the northern portion of Lyme and Black Point on the coast, was soon being poached and encroached on.

There are records of Nehantic complaints against the English from as early as May 1684, when Chief Obed petitioned the court to address English possession of the land. By 1734, the situation had grown so dire that the Nehantics were willing to make a deal. They would hear the Christian sermons of Lyme's first society reverend, Jonathan Parsons, and the east society's George Griswold in exchange for a cessation of encroachment on their land. Parsons and Griswold were distressed that the thirty native families in Lyme resisted conversion to Christianity, and most "continue in their heathenism."

Where their theological arguments failed to persuade, Parsons and Griswold used more worldly means. In their May 9, 1734 memorial to the governor and representatives at the general court in Hartford, the reverends reported, "Their chiefs told us that they would not be concerned with one religion or have a school unless the English would deal honestly with the respecting [of] their land." "They supposed that the English, their neighbors, had encroached on their property," and "they generally signified to us that if they could have the bounds of the land settled, they would willingly hear a sermon."

English assurances were empty promises, as by 1762, they were encroaching on the Black Point reservation. Nehantic complaints of

English using their land and allowing their livestock to roam free and destroy their crops led to a "compromise" when the colonial court divided the Black Point reservation into three one-hundred-acre tracts. The two southernmost tracts would remain Nehantic, but the upper one hundred acres would be divided between the Indians and the English. The justification was that in the upper one hundred acres, conflicting deeds made ownership unclear. The court maintained that John and Joseph Bull held title to this part of the Black Point reservation before it was deeded to the Nehantics, and the Bulls then sold it to Nehemiah Smith of Groton, which clouded title to the tract that's exact boundaries were in dispute. The court's decision was a Solomonic splitting of the land down the middle, with the Nehantics retaining possession of the western half of the upper one hundred, while the English interests would take title to the eastern half. The traditional Nehantic burial ground, however, was in the eastern half of the upper one hundred, and the English promised that it would be maintained as sacred land. The agreement of April 15, 1762, assures the Nehantics of "the perpetual use of their burying place, which is on that part of said tract, to bury their dead."

Archaeological digs throughout the twentieth century revealed that the Black Point burial ground, while perhaps the largest and most sacred to the tribe, was not the only one. Like English hamlets and family estates, each Nehantic village had its own burial ground. Significant finds and excavations by Norris L. Bull and William O. Beebee, along with others by Henry L. Harrison and Edward Rogers, were the first attempts by scholars to understand the life and culture of the ancient Algonquin tribes. The Charles R. Tubbs Farm, a parcel of land south of Saunders Point Road in East Lyme, was excavated by Bull and Beebee and providing evidence of fifty burials from a four-hundred-year period. It yielded numerous artifacts, including awls, needles, harpoons and fishhooks made of bone, as well as pottery shards, steatite bowls and quartz arrowheads.

At Griswold Point, several graves were found. A dig by the Yale Peabody Museum in the summers of 1939 and 1940 uncovered two graves—one of a mother holding her baby in her arms and another of a warrior holding a stone in his hand, with a bone dagger resting on his forehead. Enormous shell heaps composed primarily of oyster but also quahog, scallop and razor clam shells, along with acorns and walnuts, were also discovered, revealing the diet and industry of the Nehantics. Traces of firepits on the site offered evidence of Nehantic methods of preserving oysters by smoking them, providing sustenance through the winter months. Also found were drinking

Wading River points

Arrowheads found at Old Lyme. *Yale University / public domain.*

cups made of conch and clam shell and jewelry, such as bone pendants and animal teeth suspended from cords of hair.

The report issued from the Peabody dig indicated that there were previous digs, including one by Norris Bull in 1922. Though Bull "took no field notes," the numerous items and "skeletal material" he discovered were added to his collection of thousands of artifacts housed in the basement vault of his West Hartford home, providing the material for a private museum he would call the Connecticut Archaeological Museum and Field Survey. William O. Beebee teamed up with Bull, adding 4,500 artifacts to the collection. Much of this collection is currently housed at the University of Connecticut in Storrs.

The most shocking find, however, would take place in the1980s, when construction of a new home on Columbus Avenue unearthed Nehantic skeletons and provided a first glimpse of the extent to which the seasonal neighborhood of Crescent Beach had been built on a burial ground. This sacred site, some thirty feet above sea level and gently sloping toward Niantic Bay to within about three hundred feet of its shores, was bound by Columbus Avenue to the north, Atlantic Avenue to the east, Ocean Avenue to the south and Hillside Avenue to the west. When James V. Luce bought the last parcel of Nehantic land—the burial ground—from the State of Connecticut in 1886 and developed it into White Beach and what later became Crescent Beach, he was bound by the condition of the sale to remove the Nehantic graves to a suitable location. He removed six marked graves to Union Cemetery on Pattagansett Road, where they can be seen today. But he neglected to remove the nine hundred or so unmarked graves, which remained beneath the newly divided plots of his development. How Luce came to own and develop the burial ground, a site the State of Connecticut vowed to preserve and protect in perpetuity only a decade or so earlier, is a story in itself.

Throughout the eighteenth century, the Nehantics continued in their traditional ways despite the steady erosion of their numbers. A map drawn by Ezra Stiles of the region as he experienced it in 1761 shows "wigwams at the shore" in what is present-day downtown Niantic. To the best of their ability, the Nehantics preserved their customs, culture and way of life. They held onto their spiritual beliefs through the early eighteenth century, resisting attempts at conversion by the local Congregational ministers. It was not until the arrival of failed London actor turned firebrand evangelical preacher George Whitfield in 1741 that the Nehantics began to accept the Christian faith. Few could resist the charismatic preacher's sermons, and his acolytes, Lyme reverends Parsons and Griswold, reported that Whitefield was able to bring three hundred white and thirteen native families into the fold of the New Light Order of the Congregational Church.

Even while becoming devout Christians, the Nehantics maintained their old beliefs, syncretizing them into their newfound faith and passing them on to subsequent generations. Thus Mohegans and Nehantics in the early twentieth century could speak to anthropologist Frank Speck about Manitou, the supernatural power, life force and guardian spirit that embraces all living creatures and protects humans, and humanity's nemesis, Hobbomock, the devil, who has also been called "the author of all humans."

The distinction between good and evil, in Nehantic belief, was not absolute. Rather, all of creation was suffused with the life force that binds every creature to another and creates both the order and disorder of the universe. Creation was not divided but whole, and good and evil were only two aspects of the same force that suffuses all being. Indeed, the world was enchanted, with trees and even stones possessing an aspect of spirit. And supernatural creatures, such as Tca'namid the trickster, the "little people" called Makiawisag and Weetucks the "giant," roamed the land. The legend of Weetucks persisted into modern times. It was said that he lived around 1500, was as tall as the treetops and plucked sturgeon from the river and bears from the trees with his bare hands. He was a friend to the Indians, and when the first English ships were spotted off Pawcatuck, the Nehantics thought it was Weetucks returning. Other legends, such as Singing Rock and Lucretia's Spring, simply dealt with loss—maidens waiting in vain for their beloved's return from battle or the sea.

The Christian influence on the Nehantics, inflamed by Whitefield, was made manifest by Samson Occum, a Mohegan who became a renowned divine, drawing countless souls into the church. Educated at Eleazer Wheelock's Moor's Indian Charity School in Lebanon, Connecticut, Occum was the product of a concerted effort by colonial Connecticut authorities to educate and Christianize their "heathen" neighbors. In 1723, Captain John Mason, overseer of the Mohegans, went to live among them under the auspices of the Society for the Propagation of the Gospel, which was formed by the English Parliament in 1649. Occum was converted in 1739, and his career took him to England and Scotland, where he preached some four hundred sermons and raised £12,000 for the college Wheelock was founding. To Occum's dismay, that college became Dartmouth, which at the time, was a school dedicated to whites and excluded the likes of Occum. Disappointed in Wheelock, Occum set about creating his own community of fellow Indians who could live a devout Christian life in a place unmolested by adversarial influence. In 1775, he negotiated an agreement with the Six Nations for an ample piece of land, twenty miles square, near Oneida and established the Christian Indian community of Brotherton, New York.

For the Nehantics, who faced the prospect of a hardscrabble life on a reservation that had to be constantly tended and defended that was increasingly hemmed in by a society that treated them at best as second-class citizens in their own land, the Brotherton movement proved attractive. The degree of marginalization faced by the Nehantics is evidenced by the punishments meted out by colonial courts. One small but illuminating comparison concerns the differing penalties for public drunkenness. In October 1681, the Connecticut authorities laid down the law, stating, "For the prevention of drunckeness in Indians it is by this Court farther ordered that if any Indian be found drunk in any township in this colony, he shall be severely whipt or otherwise punished."

Going further, the judges decreed, "It is also ordered, that if any Indian taken with drink, or being found drunck doe accuse any Englishman with furnishing him with the sayd drink, then sayd person so charged shall clear himself by his oath, that he did not furnish the sayd Indian or any other Indian with sayd drinck."

In other words, anything an Indian testified to could be dismissed on the word of an Englishman. The double standard concerning drink was long established. A drunk Englishman did not face a severe whipping; rather, good old Jack the Lad on a bender may, at worst, have had to pony up a fine. In the minutes of a Lyme town meeting in 1645, it is stated, "George Chappell, for abuseing the Constable and excessive drinking, is to be bound to his good behavior and to be fined five pound." No whipping for Mr. Chappell, who got soused and attacked a cop.

The double standard of the law was not limited to drink but extended to the most essential aspects of daily life. The colony of Connecticut's 1723 Act Concerning Hunting by Indians appointed Major John Clark of Saybrook to inform the Nehantics living in Saybrook and Lyme "that they have liberty to go hunting and that they wear on their head a white list or other white thing on or round their heads for a note of distinction from our enemy." Along with being whitelisted, the Indians were informed that they shouldn't "affright any of our English." More significantly, by the same act, the Sachems were obligated to provide to the colonial authorities the names of all Indians under their dominion and, with forty-eight-hour notice, were legally bound to produce or account for the whereabouts of anyone on that list, wanted by the civil authorities. This was, in effect, a ghettoization and legal marginalization of a people in their own land.

The fault line between the English and Indian worlds had been fraught from the beginning and was highly charged with sexual attraction and political repression, which can be two sides of the same coin. One of our oldest national myths concerns the romance between John Rolfe and Matoax (Pocahontas) and the symbolic marriage, at the very founding of English dominion over America, of the native and the immigrant, the heathen and Christian, the "savage" and the "civilized," the ruler and the ruled. It is no mistake that Matoax, plucked from her native soil and transplanted to England, withered and died.

The frisson between English and Nehantic in the Lymes was no different. It informed the nervousness of preachers who sought conversion of the natives before the natives converted them. In the historic record we find Nehantics marrying into both the white and black communities. The royal line of the Nehantic Nonesuch family of the nineteenth century has examples of marriages to members of other tribes and to members of both the black and white communities, creating—in one generation—a cultural fluidity, variance in physical appearance and question of identity, that was often used against them.

The question of Indian "authenticity" as a means of marginalization came to the fore, while full-blooded Nehantics were still alive and well and could be found locally and in neighboring towns. An article in the *East Lyme Star* dated June 1, 1867, opines, "It is difficult now to tell the 'Indians of

Betsy Nonesuch. *Indian and Colonial Research Center.*

Niantic' from American citizens of African descent." This bit of editorial comment is found just below a public notice announcing a "Great Sale of Land—All the land belonging to the Niantic tribe of Indians is to be sold at auction, Tuesday, June 4th at 1 o'clock PM." The potency of the attraction and political proscription of it has been an animating force in American culture from its very outset. It is a cracked bell that is still rung in our day and age.

In 1993, a real estate developer turned casino impresario sought to overturn the gaming agreement between the State of Connecticut and the Pequot tribal nation. In his testimony to the United States Congress, Donald J. Trump said of the Nutmeg State's native population, who had been continuously living on their ancestral lands since time immemorial, "Go up to Connecticut…and you look. They don't look like Indians to me." Later, as president of the United States, he sought to diminish one of his opponents by affixing her with the sobriquet Pocahontas, setting a charge in the fault at the foundation of American culture.

The Nehantics did not live to see the age of casino development in the vicinity of the Lymes. If they had, perhaps Black Point would be a resort to rival the Mohegan Sun and the Pequot Foxwoods Casino. They were declared extinct in 1870, though members of the tribe were still very much alive. The process of "extinction" had been long in the making and was, in part, due to a loss of population that mirrored the decline of Lyme's population in general through the nineteenth century, as well as a legal definition of who was Nehantic and who wasn't—based not on lineage and genealogy, but on place of residence. Unlike an American citizen, Nehantics would lose their rights to their reservation land at Black Point if they did not live there for fifteen years. Further, state law decreed that a Nehantic marrying outside of the tribe was no longer considered a Nehantic. Thus, when Mercy Nonesuch married the Mohegan Henry Matthews, she lost her legal identity as a Nehantic and her rights to the reservation at Black Point. At Mohegan, members of the Matthews, Skeesucks and Dolbears families are Nehantic descendants.

The attrition of the Nehantic population through the late seventeenth and early eighteenth centuries was slow and steady. The estimated 400 tribal members at the time of first permanent English settlement in 1635 had fallen to 104 in 1774. Their number declined precipitously in the first half of the nineteenth century, with only 17 members in 1830 and 10 in 1849. As with non-Native Lyme residents, many went west for better opportunity, while others signed onto whaling vessels and circled the world. Samson Occum's Brotherton movement drew many Nehantics to his Oneida-area settlement. Philip Occuish, living on the Black Point reservation, converted to Christianity during the Great Awakening and became a Baptist minister. In 1799, he sent his sons to Brotherton and moved there himself in 1804. Members of the Nonesuch, Warkeet, Charles, Palmer and Poquiantup families also followed Occum to New York, and in 1832, the community relocated to Wisconsin, founding Brothertown on the shores of Lake Winnebago near Green Bay. Nehantic descendants continue to reside there today as members of the Brothertown Indian Nation.

Back home, Zaccheus Nonesuch knew that the writing was on the wall. In his petition to the State of Connecticut on May 19, 1868, he acknowledged that "reduced by death and removals only a remnant of the tribe remains. And that, in all probability, will soon be extinct." All Zaccheus asked in his petition, which was cosigned by his siblings, Anna, Betsy, John and Lucy, was that their ancestral burying ground at Black Point be preserved and "set apart as common burial place for the dead." He went on to say, "That this spot hallowed and endeared to them as the resting place of their ancestors is now a common field without protection. Your petitioners cannot believe that the State of Connecticut has ever alienated their title, or given any one permission to plow over the graves of their friends."

Plow over the graves is precisely what the state did or what James Luce did after Connecticut sold the burial ground to him in 1886. Despite the state's promise to preserve the burial ground in perpetuity after it declared the Nehantics extinct and took possession of the Black Point reservation in 1868, it took only eighteen years to break that vow. Members of the tribe who were born at Black Point, such as Mercy Nonesuch, born in a wigwam there on February 13, 1822, and Sciota Nonesuch, who was the last Nehantic born and raised on the reservation, were still very much alive.

Zaccheus Nonesuch. *Indian and Colonial Research Center.*

James Luce's new holdings, including the graveyard, became the summer resort community of Crescent Beach. A century later, the Nehantic dead who had been lost and forgotten, with cottages built over their remains, were suddenly no longer forgotten or buried, as new home construction on Columbus Avenue turned up their bones. John Pfeiffer, an Old Lyme archaeologist with extensive knowledge of the Nehantics, was called. Pfeiffer had participated in and directed numerous digs involving the Nehantics and the older sites of the Paleo-Indians who predated them. His work at the 6,000-year-old Katherine Road site in Old Lyme revealed burial practices of the first people to inhabit the Lymes. A site at the Pattagansett River excavated by Norris Bull provided evidence that the first people arrived approximately 12,500 years ago. Bull uncovered 10,000-year-old artifacts that indicated these first people were hunters of bear, caribou and mammoth. Pfeiffer's work at Katherine Road revealed that they also had a highly ritualized burial practice, which involved interring the body for a year and then exhuming the skeleton, which would be cremated and reburied with food and other provisions. Pfeiffer uncovered five thousand artifacts at the Katherine Road site, including tools and axe heads. It was natural, then, that he would be called when remains were discovered at Crescent Beach.

What Pfeiffer discovered was that the ancient Nehantic burial ground overlooking the Long Island Sound—the center of the tribe for more than 2,500 years—not only extended beyond the cleared area found in today's

McCook Park but also continued under the streets and houses of Crescent Beach, and the bodies were still interred there. James Luce only partially fulfilled his obligation to the state, removing six of the hundreds that were buried there.

The new house construction on Columbus Avenue had uncovered two sets of remains, which Pfeiffer was called to investigate. Seeing that these were Nehantic, Pfeiffer offered $2,500 of his own money to persuade the homebuilder to hold construction and give him time to investigate. Working as quickly as possible, he uncovered and removed a total of fourteen remains: ten adults, three children and one infant. He also discovered wampum and seventeenth-century European wine bottles and glass beads. To preserve the remains for research, they were brought to the state archaeologist's office.

The removal of these remains proved controversial, and MoonFace Bear of the Golden Hill Paugussett tribe objected to Pfeiffer's work, calling him "a wolf guarding the henhouse." As an activist, MoonFace Bear was involved in an armed standoff with Connecticut State Police in 1993 over the sale of untaxed cigarettes from the Paugussett's Colchester reservation.

Nehantic memorial marker, 2019. *Jim Lampos.*

In the Nehantic burial ground controversy, MoonFace Bear insisted that the remains should not be disturbed. Construction of homes and sewer projects in Crescent Beach would not be stopped though, and had Pfeiffer not stepped in, the remains and the Nehantic story they tell would have been lost forever.

While the motivations of the archaeologists may have been pure and done from a place of respect for the Nehantic people and a desire to further our understanding of them and to preserve their memory, MoonFace Bear's distrust—rooted in the centuries of broken promises and exploitation by the English, who later came to call themselves Americans—was well founded. Indeed, in his 1989 archaeological survey report conducted as part of the Crescent Beach sewer project, Kevin A. McBride noted that James Luce was not wholly ignorant of the existence of additional graves at his new beach resort after he removed the five obvious ones. "It also appears that Luce excavated a number of other Western Nehantic burials to obtain grave goods after this period," and "several documents have been located which suggest that Luce sold artifacts (grave goods) from the Crescent Beach Cemetery."

By the 1920s and '30s, these artifacts had become part of Norris Bull's collection. This implication of Bull in Luce's actions—essentially looting— tainted the reputation of future archaeologists by association, and it's easy to see how a Native American might have regarded them as grave robbers instead of scientists and scholars. In the latter part of the twentieth century, John Pfeiffer and MoonFace Bear may have had a sympathetic goal of honoring the Nehantics, but the fault line of our culture ran between them.

The exploitation of the Nehantics was not confined to a loss of land. As children, they were indentured to white families by state-appointed overseers. In many cases, this condition was little better than slavery. Girls were bound by the overseer for $50 and boys for $100. Lucretia Bogue, a Nehantic who lived from 1863 to 1952, called herself "an Indian slave girl." Her indenture at age seven to John Carpenter, a Mansfield farmer, made for an unhappy childhood where she was separated from her family and forced into involuntary labor. Nehantic children were bound to their indentured servitude until marriage.

Mercy Nonesuch, the last surviving full Nehantic, was also indentured at age seven, albeit to a more charitable mistress, Ethelinda Caulkins Griswold of Giants Neck, who provided her with an education and taught her skills such as playing the parlor organ. In 1840, Mercy's term of service expired, and she went to work for Mrs. C.C. Griswold. While Mercy gained her full freedom, she lost the birthright of her Nehantic heritage when she married Henry Matthews on March 30, 1846. Matthews would later serve as chief of the Mohegans in 1902, and by virtue of the marriage, Mercy was now considered a Mohegan.

Mercy's brother John (1817–1870), also raised as a youngster at the Black Point reservation, was indentured at age ten or twelve to Calvin Manwaring. As an adult, he farmed on the reservation but left to open a saloon on Prison Street in New London's bustling riverfront red-light district just north of the Parade. The degree to which this was a voluntary removal from the reservation is in question. A February 15, 1870 article in the *Hartford Courant* reports, "John Nonesuch, the last of the Niantic tribe of Indians, has an order from the Superior Court to sell his lands at Niantic, and is about to remove to New London." John's son Sciota married a white woman and moved to Philadelphia but maintained his Nehantic identity. Chief Sciota paid frequent visits to East Lyme and Uncasville though the 1920s to visit his ancestral homeland.

Mercy became a respected elder of the Mohegan tribe, transmitting her direct knowledge of traditions to the new generation of the twentieth century. An expert at beadwork and basketry and a source of knowledge of the gathering of plants used in herbal medicine, Mercy was cited by Gladys Tantaquidgeon as one of her three "grandmothers," along with Lydia Fielding and Emma Baker.

Gladys, who died in 2005 at the age of 106, was known the world over as the Mohegan medicine woman. In southeastern Connecticut, she and her brother, Harold "Chief Harry" Tantaquidgeon, are fondly remembered as the kindly caretakers of the charming museum at their home atop Mohegan Hill. Tenth-generation direct descendants of Uncas, Gladys and Harry dedicated their lives to preserving their culture and educating the young. Gladys did her academic work at the University of Pennsylvania, mentored by anthropologist Frank Speck, who first met her when she was a young child and he was visiting Mohegan. Gladys published ethnographies based on her personal knowledge of Mohegan ways and her field work with the Wampanoag, Sioux and Lenape people. Her accomplishments, too numerous to name here, would come as a surprise to the children from Norwich, Montville and surrounding towns, who visited her and Harry on school trips.

Harry, with his father and Gladys, built the modest fieldstone museum behind their home by hand in 1931. To the young students who came to visit, an indelible impression was made. The diminutive Gladys would begin with a talk inside the museum and then guide the students around displays in glass cases and point to pictures and artifacts on the wall. Then, outside, they

Left: Gladys Tantaquidgeon, 1931. *Indian and Colonial Research Center.*

Below: Chief Harry Tantaquidgeon, 1983. *Indian and Colonial Research Center.*

would meet Chief Harry. Harry had the demeanor of an old Yankee, with his flannel shirt and stoic way, but he had a certain kindness and warmth radiating through his flinty exterior. He would usually be found whittling, chopping wood or doing some chore around the premises. But turning his attention to us—the awed schoolchildren of neighboring towns—he would demonstrate a traditional craft, such as sourcing materials for basketmaking from the surrounding woods or the technique for making a basket sound enough that it could carry the heaviest load or even water, without a drop leaking through. This was a skill he learned from Henry Matthews, Mercy's husband. He showed us how to find saplings good for framing wigwams, how to build a firepit, traditional ways of fire making, planting and stone wall making. He taught us myriad skills that we think of as traditional to Yankee New England but have come to realize are much older and had been transmitted by the first people themselves—hand to hand, generation to generation, over thousands of years down to our own time.

And this is how we come to know the world—who we are and what we are—in a profound way that transcends ready-made definitions. When the door was open at their home and the flag was raised in the front yard—Harry was a deeply patriotic World War II veteran—passersby were welcome to stop in and say "hello." Chief Harry's demeanor was such that one wouldn't dream of abusing the privilege. He was a busy man. But his door was open, and in times of uncertainty, one could repair there, not so much for his advice but just to be in his sensible, grounding presence. To hear his words, not meted out or measured, but natural and just. A life-changing experience for the author is when Harry led him to the edge of the yard where the woods began and taught him "how to walk"—silently, without breaking a twig or rustling a leaf. It wasn't just a hunting technique; it was a way of being and seeing and living in the world. It was an appreciation of our own place in it. These terse lessons—generously passed on to the children and young adults growing up in the Thames River Valley—were gifts of immeasurable value.

And back inside the house, when Gladys gently touched your forearm to draw your attention to a particular point, you were not only feeling the direct transmission of her wisdom but also the grace of her grandmother Mercy's hand.

14

SÉANCES BY THE SHORE

The Spiritualist movement emerged in the 1840s and reached the height of its popularity in the United States during and after the Civil War. The daunting number of casualties reported from distant battlefields left countless bereft mourners back home seeking news of their beloved dead. Many people embraced Spiritualism at this time, as it offered a means to receive messages and comfort from their dearly departed.

According to tenets adopted by the National Association of Spiritualist Churches in the early twentieth century, "Spiritualism is the Science, Philosophy and Religion of continuous life, based upon the demonstrated fact of communication, by means of mediumship, with those who live in the Spirit World." Spiritualists believe "death is not the cessation of life, but mere change of condition." They believe that there is communication between this world and the spirit realm that is facilitated by "mediums," who are "able to convey messages and produce the phenomena of Spiritualism, including Prophecy, Clairvoyance, Clairaudience, Gift of Tongues, Laying on of Hands, Healing, Visions, Trance, Apports, Levitation, Raps, Automatic and Independent Writings and Paintings, Voice, Materialization, Photography, Psychometry, etc."

In 1848, sisters Margaret, Leah and Kate Fox of Hydesville, New York, began to gain fame as mediums. They were were said to be able to communicate with spirits through a series of rapping and "table knocking." Although Margaret Fox later wrote a confessional tome asserting that all of their spirit activity had been a hoax contrived through trickery, many

Spiritualists continued firmly in their beliefs. Shortly thereafter, Fox tried to take back her confession, but the sisters' reputation had already been ruined.

The Pine Grove Spiritualist Camp was established at Niantic in 1881 as a summer retreat for Spiritualists to meet and listen to speakers from around the country. Located on a strip of land between Smith Cove and the Niantic River, Pine Grove was also a place where Spiritualist families could relax and enjoy the beautiful natural surroundings and amusements offered, just as at any other summer resort. The lure of Pine Grove was the same as many of the seaside retreats that were so popular in the late nineteenth and early twentieth centuries but with an added fillip—it was a destination for devoted Spiritualists to meet away from the prying eyes and curious questions of nonbelievers. Though the Pine Grove Spiritualists were always welcoming to their secular neighbors, inviting them for dances and other activities, the camp gave its residents a sense of safety and security, where they could discuss and practice their faith in the company of fellow believers.

The camp property had previously been farmland. It was purchased by the Connecticut Spiritualist Campmeeting Association and was divided into small lots of approximately twenty-five by fifty feet. These lots were leased to members for terms of forty-nine or ninety-nine years. Initially, Pine Grove truly was a camp, as people pitched tents on their lots, but soon, cottages were built among the tall pines that lent their name (and wood) to the endeavor. These early cottages were often remarked on for their beauty and elaborate "gingerbread gothic" detailing. Set close together and painted in different colors, the rows of cottages presented a quaint and pleasant streetscape depicted in many photo postcards of the era.

On August 17, 1881, the *New York Times* announced:

> *The Spiritualists of Connecticut have bought in this place a fine tract of land, which is mostly included in a beautiful pine grove, for a permanent camp-meeting ground, and it is to be occupied for the first time with services tomorrow....The situation of the land is very attractive for the purpose designed. Upon the east side is the Niantic River, which is navigable for small boats for about four miles above the Niantic Bay, and upon the west side is a small fresh water lake deep enough for good sailing. Between these waters is the central part of the camp meeting ground, upon a knoll covered with pines, now well cleared so as to define the several streets which have already been laid out. Over 150 lots have already been sold, and some cottages are now being erected. By another season there will be extensive building. An ornamental speaker's stand has been built on the east side of*

Pine Grove cottages, 1905. *Connecticut Spiritualist Camp Meeting Association.*

Pine Grove speakers' stand, circa 1895. *Connecticut Spiritualist Camp Meeting Association.*

the grounds in a spot where is a natural amphitheatre, and seats are ranged in this shady grove covering it. It is intended to make the place a resort for Connecticut Spiritualists of which there are several thousand in the state.... At the present meeting, several prominent speakers will be present as well as many well-known mediums.

Pine Grove grew rapidly, and members drew up covenants and chore rotations to share the labor of keeping the camp clean and pleasant. On August 22, 1887, the *Hartford Courant* reported that services to dedicate a new tabernacle, "a neat building with a seating capacity for two or three hundred situated at the western edge of the grounds," had taken place at Pine Grove the previous Thursday. It stated that "many cottages are rapidly filling, and next week will see them all occupied, when with favorable weather, the distinguished D.D.s will have large crowds to address." The "distinguished D.D.s" (doctors of divinity, reverends, et cetera) were a major draw at Pine Grove. Believers could attend Spiritualist services and lectures on topics of interest that were led by the popular divines and mediums of the day. Some of the lectures and meetings were open to the public as a way to spread the message of Spiritualism to the larger community.

A Pine Grove landmark, which is preserved only in souvenir postcards, was known as "Burnham's Folly." This was a one-hundred-foot-tall wooden observation tower built by a Mr. L.H. Burnham, who charged a small fee for people to climb the tower and see the view from the top. The "folly" designation came from the fact that after one had paid the admission fee and made the arduously steep climb to the top, there was no reason to repeat the experience, so admissions and interest quickly diminished. The tower itself fell victim to a fierce windstorm in 1914 and came crashing down to earth, crushing a (fortunately uninhabited) cottage.

It is interesting to note that Pine Grove had a very cordial relationship with the military enclave next door, which had been purchased by the State of Connecticut as a training camp for the National Guard. Unlike the well-fortified base that is there today, there was no fence between the National Guard and Pine Grove. After the United States officially entered World War I, soldiers became an increasingly common sight on the country roads, as their companies practiced hard marching with heavy packs.

On September 14, 1917, the *Hartford Courant* dramatically proclaimed, "Sons of Mars Will Dance at Pine Grove," stating, "There will be a social in the dance hall at Pine Grove to which soldiers are especially invited. Dancing will start at 7.30 and festivities will continue until 9.40 as soldiers

Pine Grove temple and speakers' stand, 2019. *Michaelle Pearson.*

must be in camp before taps." These mixers were fondly recalled by Pine Grove residents for many years thereafter. Olive Tubbs Chendali related that Pine Grove remained a very social place, with a pavilion for dancing, a dining hall, tennis courts and a ballfield. It even had its own fire station and general store with a post office.

Pine Grove was devastated by the hurricane of 1938. The stately black pitch pines were uprooted, and many cottages were destroyed or severely damaged, but residents cleaned up and rebuilt their cottages, and by the 1940s, homes began to be owned by families who were not affiliated with the Spiritualist temple. Residents eventually sued for the right to own their land rather than lease it. They won this right, but all common grounds and waterfront, with rare exception, remain the property of the Connecticut Spiritualist Campmeeting Association.

Today, Pine Grove is a picturesque community with both year-round and summer residents. There is a nursery project underway to restore the historic black pitch pines, which is headed by the Oswegatchie Hills Nature Preserve. The Spiritualist temple is open seasonally from June to September and features lectures and workshops with noted mediums, healers and Spiritualist teachers, in addition to regularly scheduled worship services and readings.

15

THE MOST BEAUTIFUL GRANITE

The granites of the Lymes were known far and wide for their beauty, durability and strength. The stones of each town were different in composition, and each was suited for different applications. The purplish gray variegated Lyme granite gneiss found at Joshua's Rock and the Mamacoke gneiss of Selden Island were both prized for sturdy building blocks and for the cobblestones that paved the streets of New York City. The "Golden Pink" of Niantic and reddish "McCurdy Pink" porphyritic granite of Old Lyme were initially used for decorative motifs, such as carved details or columns, where their unusual colors could be shown to best advantage. However, both the Golden Pink and McCurdy granites were later selected for use as building blocks for particular projects where the architect or builder was seeking a more dramatic use of the stone.

The most famous of the early quarries in East Lyme was started by Samuel Smith in Oswegatchie Hills in 1815. According to the East Lyme Historical Society (ELHS), the initial purpose of the quarry was to provide stone for a house Smith was building at Smith's Cove, but it also provided stone for other endeavors, such as the 1831 Stone Church on Society Road.

The Stone Church (now referred to as the "Old Stone Church") was abandoned in 1879 and demolished soon after, but some of its granite blocks were used to build the fireplace of the Main Street library in Niantic during the early 1920s. The ELHS also noted the late 1800s discovery of "a vein of golden pink granite along the ridge above Riverview Road, from the Old Stone Church Burial Ground, south."

The Old Stone Church, East Lyme. *East Lyme Historical Society.*

From 1860 through 1910, the quarries of Lyme, Old Lyme and East Lyme were booming industries that employed thousands of workers. They were self-contained ecosystems that not only required skilled stonemasons imported from Italy, England and Ireland but also all manner of laborers to provide support for the work. These included blacksmiths, diggers, drillers, cooks, wagon drivers, mechanics, carters and entry-level workers with strong backs to haul debris and load the quarried blocks onto carts, railcars and ships. Many of these quarries were located as close to water as possible to allow the blocks to be loaded onto vessels and shipped directly to ports, such as New York, which had a seemingly endless appetite for granite cobblestones and building blocks. The other primary means of transport was the railroad, which came through Old Lyme and East Lyme in the 1850s.

Nelson Dale and Herbert E. Gregory, writing for the U.S. Geological Survey in 1911, gave details of more modern quarries in East Lyme, chief among them the Malnati Pink quarry and the Carlson quarry, both of which transported stone by cart approximately two miles to Niantic. Each of these quarries specialized in stone for monuments.

The Malnati Pink quarry was located two miles northwest of Niantic station and 160 feet above it. The operator is listed as Angelo Malnati of Quincy, Massachusetts. The granites mined there were known as "Golden Pink Niantic" and a deeper hued "Golden Pink Dark." Dale and Gregory noted, "The quarry, opened in 1900, measures about 250 feet from east to west by 65 feet across and 75 feet in depth." Further records tell that "the plant comprises two derricks, a hoisting engine, a steam drill, a vertical polisher and engine for same, and two steam pumps."

The Carlson quarry also opened in 1900, a mere six hundred feet southwest of Malnati, and its granite was of the same structure, appearance and composition. The operator is listed as the Golden Pink Quarry Co., and Peter M. Carlson of Niantic is listed as the proprietor. This quarry measured about 125 by 75 feet and from 10 to 30 feet deep. The equipment is listed as one hand and one steam derrick and engine, as well as a steam pump.

Selden Island, known formally as "Selden Neck State Park" is a "maritime state park" in Lyme and is accessible only by water. It was formerly known as the "Twelve Mile Farm" and "Lord's Island" and did not become an island until 1854, when an unexpectedly strong spring freshet caused severe flooding. This rush of water devastated the fishing fleet, deposited massive quantities of silt and cut a new channel, creating an island. At approximately 607 acres, Selden is Connecticut's largest island and home to one of the earliest colonial settlements, which was granted in 1652 to Captain John Cullick, who had been secretary of the colony of Connecticut and helped facilitate the merging of Saybrook Colony into the Connecticut Colony. Cullick never lived on Selden Island and sold his holdings there to John Leveritt in 1691. A few years later, in 1696, Leveritt sold to Joseph Selden of Hadley, Massachusetts, who began cultivating the island, mainly as grazing for livestock. The State of Connecticut began purchasing land in 1917, but Selden descendants retained some property on the island until 1976.

In the 1880s, quarry companies based in Manhattan and Brooklyn, New York, began working the island, bringing hordes of workers and machinery to harvest the granite. In August 1891, the *Deep River New Era* published an article touting the success of the granite quarrying operation at Selden Island. It stated that the capacity of the site was 3,500 blocks per day but was expected to grow rapidly with the addition of more workers and machinery:

> *At present the cutters are working on a very large contract for stone which is to be used for the gate house on the great Croton aqueduct at Croton Lake in New York State. The gate house, will, when finished, be the largest in the world. It is about 110 feet square, the front being of cut stone and the north, south and west elevations of smooth stone. The company also has another contract for a million and one-half paving stone, to be used for Surf Avenue, one of the principal streets at Coney Island.*

The granite was known for its beauty and strength, and the company engaged I.H. Woolston at the School of Mines, Columbia College, to test it. Woolston wrote, "The stone taken from Lord's Island is the Brotite [Biotite] Hornblend [sic] variety, and the combination of the clear feldspar with the black brotite gives the granite its red color. The rocks on the west side of the river are of a different variety, called Muscovite-Hornblend, containing some garnet."

The most famous quarry in Old Lyme was the McCurdy quarry located at McCurdy Road on the Duck River and owned by Judge Charles McCurdy. Noted for its rich reddish pink color, specimens of this pegmatite granite were shown at the Philadelphia Exposition in 1876 and the Paris Exhibition in 1878. Professor W.B. Blake wrote of the Paris exhibits for the *Hartford Courant* in 1879:

> *The rose colored coarsely crystalline granite from the quarry of the Honorable Charles J. McCurdy of Old Lyme was shown by a beautifully polished block. This stone is remarkable for the beauty of its crystalline aggregation and the color, in both respects closely resembling the anciently quarried and worked Egyptian Granite which we find examples of in the pyramids and in the collections of the Louvre. The polished surfaces derive an additional beauty from the translucency and pearly lustre of the large feldspar crystals, seen to best advantage in strong sunlight. There is*

a peculiar chatoyant gleam reminding one of the gems known as cats' eyes. All these qualities render this a peculiarly beautiful and valuable stone for ornamental work, it being equally suitable for pedestals and columns. It was greatly admired by the jury, and by the distinguished Chief of the Government School of Mines, M. Daubrée. The jury decreed an Honorable Mention and diploma.

Monsieur D'Aubrée described the stone as "remarkable for the distinctness of the crystallization, isolating the feldspar, quartz and mica one from the other."

Judge McCurdy was clearly conflicted about mining this quarry. His personal correspondence, held by the Old Lyme Historical Society (OLHSI), reflects both an ambition to promote the unusual qualities of the stone and a certain reluctance to extract it for less than a substantial premium over other regionally available granites. McCurdy sent samples to geologists, schools of mining and natural history museums, collecting their opinions and publishing a pamphlet of these testimonials in an effort to interest a third party into taking over the mining operations, so he could reap the benefits of ownership while leaving the actual extraction, carving and carting to a "suitable professional." Writing for himself and his son-in-law E.E. Salisbury, who was his partner in the quarry, McCurdy stated plainly, "[W]e will do all we can but we are not quarry men or stone contractors. Our object is to place the business in the hands of those who are familiar with its requirements, its risks and its profits."

McCurdy sent samples of his stone to the committee charged with building the Channing Memorial Church in Newport, Rhode Island, as a memorial to Unitarian Universalist founder and abolitionist William Ellery Channing. The committee selected the McCurdy granite above all others, but the prize was nearly lost due to haggling over terms. It seems that the good judge had an overly optimistic view of his quarry's readiness and capacity and of the potential value of his stone in the marketplace. A flurry of firmly worded letters flew back and forth betwixt Newport and Lyme, debating the price per ton, the merits of freightage by boat and other difficulties. At one point, the committee suggested that McCurdy should consider substantially discounting the stone, as his quarry would receive substantial publicity if the stone was used for the church:

We like the stone very much, and should be pleased to have the Church built of it—and if built of it—it would advertise the stone better than any way else and the removal of 500 tons of stone from the quarry at the present time would be of exceeding value to the quarry for any future use and develop it into such shape that parties might be more willing to put capital into it. For that reason, if you should furnish the stock for the bare cost of labor and transportation it would more than pay in benefit to the quarry.

McCurdy was less than pleased by this and countered that he estimated the price per ton at approximately thirteen dollars at a time when granites from New Hampshire were selling at around five dollars per ton.

Fortunately, the committee was convinced that no other stone would do for the church building, and McCurdy, who wanted the distinction of having his granite used for such an illustrious purpose, adjusted his price accordingly. With equitable terms agreed on, the granite was to be quarried and conveyed by boat to Newport. All's well that ends well. The *Newport News* of December 18, 1880 stated:

It was through the generosity of Judge McCurdy of Connecticut that the committee were able to contract for the building of Memorial Church out of the beautiful porphyritic granite from the quarry in [Old] Lyme, Conn. This granite is of a warm, rich carnation-red or rose color, and is very remarkable for the large proportion of opalescent crystals of feldspar it contains; it resembles the red granite of Scotland and the famous Syenite of Egypt, but by distinguished chemists and geologists has been pronounced even more beautiful and equally durable.

One month later, the *Newport Mercury* concurred: "As the building approaches completion, it completely justifies the judgment of the committee who at once selected from the specimens offered the rich red porphyritic granite of Judge McCurdy." The McCurdy granite is similar to "Egyptian syenite, but with [more] warmth of color, kaleidoscopic mingling of its constituents, the chatoyant gleams of its crystals and ability to take a high polish."

The use of the McCurdy granite to build the Channing Memorial Church did result in an increased profile for the stone. In 1882 alone, the judge received numerous enquiries seeking "granite similar in quality and character as that used for the Channing Memorial Church." But after the church had been completed, he lost his enthusiasm for the quarry business, and the McCurdy granite was only used for occasional projects.

Katharine Ludington, in her memoir, *Lyme and Our Family*, remarked that Judge McCurdy "was very proud of a vein of pinkish red granite that ran through his property and wished his monument to be built of it. He never quarried it in any quantity because he did not want to tear up his land." After Judge McCurdy's death in 1891, he got his wish. His distinctive grave marker at Old Lyme's Duck River Cemetery features a large capstone of McCurdy Pink granite from his quarry.

16

THE EGYPTIAN LOTUS OF LYME

The art and mythology of ancient Egypt have influenced the Western world since at least the mid-eighteenth century. Archaeologists and adventurers launched expeditions to excavate Egypt's fabled tombs and treasures, and all things Egyptian were deemed the height of fashion. The lotus was one of the most popular Egyptian motifs. According to Egyptian mythology, the first lotus flowers bloomed from the muddy silt of the "before time" and served as a vessel for the birth of the sun god. Because lotus flowers open each morning and close in the evening, they symbolize the sunrise and rebirth. Napoleon's troops drew maps and plans of the Valley of the Kings, and by the early 1800s, Western architects, decorators and artisans began incorporating Egyptian revival styles into their work—to the point where the craze became known as "Egyptomania." The fascination with all things Egyptian continued throughout the nineteenth and early twentieth centuries, reaching another high point with the discovery of King Tutankhamen's tomb in 1922.

This interest in all things Egyptian reached even the small Connecticut hamlet of Lyme. On September 14, 1894, the *Hartford Courant* wrote of a "beautiful bed of an oriental water flower, the Egyptian lotus, famed in song and story" that could be seen blooming in Selden's Cove on the Connecticut River. The flowers are described as "very fragrant and beautiful," resembling the pond lily "but of much larger proportion....The leaves resemble lily pads and measure from eighteen to twenty five inches in diameter."

An 1882 feature from the *Middletown Constitution* described the Selden Cove lilies, stating, "The leaves are about two feet in diameter and about two acres of water are covered with them. The blossom is a pure white, the bud is about the size of a tulip, but when open the flower is nearly as large as the night blooming cereus. Inside are a number of seeds as large as orange seeds."

However beautiful this bed of lilies may have been, its fame as a sightseeing attraction was chiefly due to some quite fanciful tales as to how the flowers may have journeyed from far-off Africa. The *Courant* article says, "Some think that the seeds were brought here in a cargo of rags which came from Egypt years ago." Local residents enthusiastically embellished these romantic notions, connecting the lovely lilies of Lyme with the mysteries of the ancient world, claiming that the seeds must have been brought on ships by enterprising merchants who used discarded mummy wrappings that tomb vandals had left behind to cushion crates of goods shipped from Egypt.

Folklorist Stephen Gencarella detailed several of these legends in an article for *Connecticut Explored* magazine. He noted that these accounts often featured an unnamed narrator, such as an article in the *Deep River New Era*, which cites "a doctor from Essex," who "went hunting in Selden Cove" and "discovered enormous lily pads from which a purplish-white blossom emerged, far greater in size than he had ever seen." The doctor then asked "a friend knowledgeable in botany," and the two concluded "that the specimen fit only the description of the Egyptian lotus, a native plant of the Nile River."

A paper-industry trade publication titled *Rags in Paper* picked up the story of the lotus in 1928. Its version contains many of the familiar elements, citing "an old resident of the Connecticut Valley, who prefers to be anonymous" as the source of the tale. *Rags* stated that the discoverer of the esteemed flower was a doctor from Essex who was hunting game in Seldon's Cove and described "purplish white blossoms that were far bigger and more beautiful than any water-lily of his experience." It goes on to describe the doctor's exhaustive search through hefty botanical volumes aided by a trusty, but equally anonymous, friend, cited only as a "minister" and "noted botanist."

These two concluded, based on their reading, that the flower in question must be "the famed Egyptian Lotus flower—the giant Lily of the Nile." Colorful details are supplied as to the supposed origins of the lotus, making a connection to the rags used in paper making: "New England sea captains, venturing into sun-scorched harbors along the North African coast, found cargo after cargo of Egyptian linens that had been old in the days of Rameses and which by custom had been placed in bundles in the tombs for use of the departed spirits.…The Yankee skippers…knew it would make good paper. They filled their holds with these cloths and robes of forgotten kings and queens and sailed away to America."

A romantic picture is painted of the unloading of the precious cargo in Connecticut: "We can picture lanky longshoremen heaving bales of the ancient stuff out onto the docks…a warm wind blowing up from the Sound; a light tide rippling in around the old green piling. Out of those bundles fell dust, like old lavender of today, that was the seeds of sacred flowers, entombed ages ago. The South breeze carried it gently into the river. And so, by whim of chance, the seeds of the lotus floated on an eddy of the tide into the broad inner reaches of Seldon's cove."

Thanks to these and other published accounts, the fame of the Egyptian Lotus of Lyme spread far and wide, and versions of how the lilies came to be in Selden's Cove were as colorful and varied as the locals could make them. Seasonal tourists from as far away as New York and Boston descended on the quiet cove to see the flowers, providing a tidy sum for enterprising watermen along the Connecticut River, who were willing to forego a day's fishing to guide deep-pocketed sightseers on botanical expeditions.

Gencarella concluded, "The Selden Cove lotus does have a basis in reality. As early as the 1840s botany manuals recognized that the plant in question was the American lotus (*Nelumbium luteum*) or the water chinquapin." This is a logical explanation and most likely the truth of the matter.

The botanical journal *Meehan's Monthly* noted in 1896 that "the New World representative of the famous Egyptian Lotus is said to grow abundantly in Selden's Cove, near Lyme, Connecticut," which seems to support this conclusion. But we may never know for sure, as local accounts state that the lotus bed was washed away in a storm. Still, the memory of the Egyptian Lotus of Lyme lives on in the popular imagination, perpetuated by a romantic notion that Selden's Cove may once have been home to an exotic wonder from Egyptian shores.

17

Bring on the Diving Horses

There was a convergence of three factors that led to the "discovery" of the Connecticut Shoreline by the "summer crowd": the expansion of the railroads provided an inexpensive and efficient means for people to escape the heat of the city for the cool breezes of the coast; labor reforms allowed working people to have more leisure time; and the popular belief that time spent at the shore was healthy for warding off the miasma of disease from the crowded, sweltering cities. At first, the Victorian shore resorts were the exclusive province of the wealthy, but with each passing year, they became more attainable to the general public.

Atlantic City, New Jersey, and Coney Island, New York, began as luxury resorts for wealthy holidaymakers but soon attracted all classes of people and many more day trippers, due to greater accessibility by trolley and railroad. In Connecticut, the development of the shoreline followed a similar timeline. In 1892, Old Lyme's Sound View was developed as a genteel resort accessible by rail from Hartford, and East Lyme's Pine Grove Spiritualist Camp was founded in 1881. There were many activities to keep the summer visitors entertained—shore dinners, picnic excursions, moonlight sails, whist parties, "ghost parties" and the occasional traveling carnival. In 1905, a new destination emerged, drawing patrons from near and far: the Golden Spur Amusement Park.

The venue was founded by the owners of the East Lyme Street Railway, which operated a trolley that ran between New London and East Lyme. East Lyme historian Olive Tubbs Chendali remembered the trolley, which was also called the "East Lyme Electric Railway." In *Stories of East Lyme*, she recounted, "The basic fare was five cents per zone…commuter tickets of 80 were $3, while school tickets were 25 cents to a book for seventy-five cents."

The trolley line did a booming business during the week, serving commuters between the two towns, but there was a significant decrease in ridership on the weekend. Clearly a destination was needed that could increase ridership on these slower days. The owners chose "the Head of the River," which had once been a thriving commercial site and home to the Beckwith shipyard for their new destination park, and Ye Golden Spur was born.

Upon hearing about the Golden Spur today, most people assume it must have had some kind of Western connotation, as in the type of boot spurs worn by ranchers. It is often asked if the Golden Spur was a rodeo show, like Buffalo Bill's Wild West. As entertaining as that possibility might have been, the name stems not from the type of entertainment to be found at the park but rather from its patrons' means of arrival.

In railroad parlance, a "spur" is a small, specialized branch line that was used to serve a single client, usually a factory or shipping destination. These spurs were typically very small, with only a ten to twelve car capacity, unlike today's industrial spurs, which serve the same purpose but are much larger. When the East Lyme Street Railway proprietors designed their destination amusement venue, they hoped it would reap weekend gold (or at least cash), so it was only natural that they should it call it the "Golden Spur," as they envisioned it as a way of making the otherwise slow weekends profitable.

The park offered a kaleidoscopic array of amusements for visitors. It had a skating rink, carousel and funhouse. Popular bands played at the dance hall, and patrons could rent boats and canoes to spend the day on the water. There was a fashionable Japanese-style tearoom complete with pagoda, and rooms to let at the Golden Spur Inn and Annex for those who preferred a more extended holiday. A sign outside the Fun Parlor showcased the motto, "Who Enters Here Leaves Gloom Behind."

A postcard mailed in 1910 featured the following promotional copy, which paints an enticing picture of the delights to be found at Ye Golden Spur:

> *Golden Spur park is pleasantly situated at the head of Niantic River, where there is safe and delightful boating and canoeing. There are also free swings under the shade of the old apple trees. Fine picnic ground free to Sunday Schools and Societies. There is a merry-go-round, fun parlor, museum, bowling, shore dinners and lunch; ice cream and confectionery are on sale. Dancing with a fine orchestra. Moving pictures, afternoon and evening, free*

Diving horse "Queen" at Golden Spur Amusement Park. *East Lyme Historical Society.*

to patrons of the trolley, and other pleasant and innocent amusements. East Lyme trolley leaves State Street, New London and Niantic, ten minutes before and twenty minutes after the hour during the season.

Caro Weir Ely wrote that artist Henry Ward Ranger rented a house for the summer near Golden Spur, until he was "urged by a friend to come to Lyme, with the suggestion that Miss Florence Griswold, who lived in a big, white pillared house, might take him in. That proved to be the beginning of a dozen years of the gayest, hardest-working artist's Paradise New England has ever produced." One wonders what might have become of the Lyme art colony had Ranger decided to remain at Golden Spur!

National and regional traveling acts were featured on a rotating basis throughout the summer season. These were heavily advertised and drew many visitors to the park. Most fondly remembered of these seems to have been a pair of diving horses owned by a J.W. Gorman. These horses, named King and Queen, dove into the water from a high platform and were perennial favorites at Golden Spur. Postcards and photos of King and Queen mid-leap were popular souvenirs.

Unfortunately, the demise of the trolley and the increasing popularity of the automobile spelled the end of an era for Golden Spur. It closed in 1924 but is still remembered fondly as a favorite chapter of East Lyme history.

18

A Gungy Journal

Driving up Gungy Road to the ancient Nehantic hunting grounds in the northeast corner of Lyme, one realizes that time is not linear. The past and the future often overlap in surprising ways—things have a funny way of persisting well past their day. It's a quick ride from Golden Spur at the headwaters of the Niantic River up Whistletown to Grassy Hill and Gungy Road. Here we see bedrock tossed asunder as we climb the ridge toward the Honey Hill Fault and streams, like the aptly named Beaver Brook, blocked by watertight dams not created by the industry of man. We see stone walls, some following colonial property lines and others dating back to the Algonquins' tenure, created for what purpose we can only surmise.

It's a historian's delight, this landscape, with stands of black birch, their leaves turning lemon yellow in autumn—and mighty scarlet oaks growing up against quartz exposures. There's a quaint Congregational church here and a three-hundred-year-old home there, with smoke curling from the chimney making it all seem quintessentially New England in a nearly surreal way. It is holding back the maw of the modern age that churns and chews up the land along the Northeast Corridor from Boston to New York, extracting value and leaving it all to waste. Here, in this quiet breathing space with only the eagle's call and streams singing their way down to the Connecticut River and Long Island Sound, one is as likely to see a bear as another human, and the hand of time has passed very lightly indeed.

Joseph Caples with his carriage, Grassy Hill Road, Lyme. *Lyme Public Hall and Local History Archives.*

Maybe it shouldn't be a surprise that in this quiet corner, the voice of Joseph A. Caples—a character transcending time, a man as practical and useful as any could be, making a sport of boundaries and dancing along the fault lines of our culture—rings soft and true if we wish to listen.

Joseph Caples wrote down his family history and, as a consequence, his own life story and a history of the Gungy tract in Lyme, in 1949, a few years before his passing. "Any who had an interest in genealogy," he wrote, "will find that Truth is really stranger than fiction." The Caples family tree is predominately Nehantic but also African American—both emancipated slave and free-born—and white, including English, Irish, German, Spanish and Portuguese. Lest one think the Caples family was far-flung, most of these associations occurred in and around Lyme.

In the census records, Joseph Caples is called a mulatto, but as one reads the story written in his own clear hand, one quickly realizes that the term doesn't tell us much. He cannot be reduced to a demographic statistic, and if he is to stand as a symbol, it would be for all of the values that Lyme holds dear—hard work and industry, forthrightness, practicality, tolerance, humor and, above all, adherence to tradition and a lineage to antiquity. Among Lyme's celebrated diary, journal and genealogy writers, such as Katharine Ludington, Moses Warren and Sylvanus Griswold, Joseph Caples and his family have some of the deepest roots in the land.

A cursory glance at two of Caples's great-grandfathers, Prince Crosley and Cuff Condol, reveals a complex and multifaceted story whose various threads are woven into the tapestry of Lyme's history in surprising ways. Prince Crosley was born in Lyme circa 1754 and was baptized in the Congregational church on August 24, 1755. Thought to be the son of Governor Matthew Griswold's slave York and Eunice Crosley, a Native American, Prince was raised as a slave on the Griswold estate and, as such, his last name was originally Griswold. In 1777, he enlisted as a soldier during the Revolutionary War and served in Colonel Josiah Storr's First Regiment of the Continental Line. He was given an honorable discharge at the end of the war, in 1782, and in exchange for his patriotic service was freed from the bondage of slavery. Many slaves earned their freedom this way and, as veterans of the Revolution, helped establish postcolonial communities of free black citizens throughout New England. On earning his freedom, Prince changed his name from Griswold to Crosley and married Caroline Miller (Brockway), whom Caples notes was white.

Cuff Condol has often been referred to as a slave in the historic record, though Caples called him the "serf lad known as Cuff." His freedom was purchased in 1787 by three individuals—Sara Silas (Cyrus) and Joseph Pomham, who were both Nehantic, and Daniel Wright, who in some accounts is described as Nehantic and in others as African American. It is thought that Cuff was perhaps not born into slavery but into servitude, and Joseph Caples's description of Cuff as being "a serf" would, in that case, be more apt than the more usual term "slave" associated with him, and the three who purchased his freedom were most likely his kin. Cuff bought his freedom by repaying his three benefactors and taking up residence in the Nehantic hunting tract along Gungy Road, where he married and had several children. His son Daniel Condol married Lucy Crosley, one of Prince Crosley's daughters. Daniel Condol became a significant landowner in the Gungy tract, buying and selling lots for their wood resources. He was an expert hewer of ship's timber and a stonemason. He bought a home on Gungy Road in 1830, and it is in that house that Joseph Caples, the journal-writer, was born and raised and lived his life of quiet distinction.

The continuity of Joseph Caples's family in that corner of Lyme through the nineteenth and early twentieth centuries, when the town was suffering a loss of population and stagnant economy, was due to the fact that they were tied to the land through ownership. Like the other founding families, such as the Griswolds, Brockways and Elys, the Caples remained in Lyme because they had an economic stake in the town. For those not bound to the land, economic opportunity beckoned aboard whaling ships, in the newly settled farmlands of the Midwest, in California's gold-bearing hills and in the burgeoning industrial cities along newly laid rail lines. Lyme was being bypassed, and its old reputation as a dynamic center of economic activity and political leadership was slowly fading. It was becoming a backwater—resistant to the railroad and slow to change. Families kept their old ways, and the modern world was held at such an arm's length that an 1876 *Harper's Magazine* article describes Old Lyme as having "a fascinating air of easy old-fashioned elegance," and the town's portrait in that article is still easily recognizable. Old-fashioned ways were even more preserved in Lyme's rural northeast corner, which today rewards visitors with beautiful natural landscapes, working farms and bucolic villages.

Joseph Caples's account of his daily life in 1949 would be recognizable to his ancestors a hundred years or even two hundred years prior. Indeed, some of his work, such as the gathering of wild-growing medicinal plants, is based on the ancient wisdom of his Nehantic ancestors that spans millennia. He writes of gathering boneset, which reduces fevers and treats influenza; horehound, which is prescribed for coughs and colds; and sweetfern, which can be used as a poison wash. He gathered pennyroyal, and in Dark Hollow between Mount Archer and Whittle Rock, he would look for wild American ginseng, a valuable native plant still used today to treat myriad ills. Reading this portion of Caples's journal is not unlike reading Gladys Tantaquidgeon's work on traditional Native American remedies. The clarity of Caples's writing makes the reader's eye keener in spotting these plants still growing in the places he mentions.

Along with gathering wild herbs, Caples made his living in a variety of traditional ways. His businesses included shearing sheep, chopping cordwood and hewing ties. He hunted partridge, quail, woodcock, wild duck, squirrel and rabbit, which he shipped to New Haven. He trapped otter, mink, muskrat, raccoon, weasel and the rare lynx for fur. He also had a trained ox team for his farm, which he hired out to others who needed heavy labor done. He even worked as a barber, cutting hair for the famous artists of Lyme, all while making sport of their beards.

Joseph Caples with his ox, Grassy Hill Road, Lyme. *Lyme Public Hall and Local History Archives.*

Reminiscing about his parents, Caples notes that neither his father nor his mother had ridden in a car, seen an airplane, listened to the radio or spoken on the telephone. Caples remarks that he did not presently have electricity or even running water but had to draw it daily from a well across the street from his home. It is interesting to remember that in 1932, before the Roosevelt administration's national electrification project, only 10 percent of rural households in the United States had access to electricity, and even in sections of Lyme, this condition persisted until the mid-twentieth century. Caples's parents were skilled in crafts suited to this era of no electric light or refrigeration—his mother made hand-dipped candles and picked and preserved blueberries and huckleberries. His father gathered corncobs and hickory chips to stoke the fire in the family's kitchen fireplace and smoke hams and bacon. The family house had three fireplaces, which were not only used for cooking but also the primary sources of heat. Fishing provided the basis for many family meals, with pickerel and perch readily caught in Norwich and Hog Ponds, while Beaver Brook was known as the best trout stream. Caples remembers the regular foxhunts neighbors engaged in, and Beaver Brook was also the site of Joseph Beebee's shingle mill, where "Uncle

Joe" with his long gray beard, spectacles and "jolly smile and kind greeting" would be busy making shingles from hickory. Farther up Beaver Brook were cranberry bogs and a fulling mill. Caples reminisces about sawmills and paper mills on the Eight Mile River and gristmills near Hamburg. It was a world little removed from the dawn of the Industrial Age in the late seventeenth century.

Joseph Caples, like Mercy Nonesuch, was a conduit to the earliest parts of Lyme's history. Just as Mercy was well remembered by Gladys Tantaquidgeon, who died in 2005, there are those alive today who personally knew Joseph Caples or were taught Sunday school by him at the Grassy Hill Congregational Church. His world is still alive and with us, just as the contributions of African Americans and Nehantics join those of European heritage to create the distinctive culture that characterizes contemporary Lyme.

One must remember that, unlike much of America in the twentieth century, interracial marriages were discouraged but not illegal in colonial-era Lyme. Marriages among whites, natives and blacks occurred, and Caples notes that most venerable and ancient Lyme families may not wish to examine their family tree with too much scrutiny, lest they find noble lines that are not necessarily English. As he jokingly said of his own family, "I won't even try to trace them down too far as there are too many roons, troons, and loons to separate." With his elegant account, Caples joyfully capers on Lyme's fault line. The traces of this culture may be seen today on a ride up Gungy Road, where "the old stone walls made by Cuff and Daniel Condol will stand as a memorial for the ages as they are made of granite and will never decay."

19

THE LOOM OF THE LAND

For centuries, oxen have been used in the Lymes to perform all manner of heavy work, from drawing a plow on a farm to moving large buildings from one place to another. Some of the earliest laws of the town had to do with provisioning for oxen. The cutting of salt hay was very important as winter feed and bedding for oxen and other farm animals. It was also used as a protective outer layer atop stacks of more delicate upland hay in the fields. There are two main kinds of grass termed "salt hay": salt hay grass (*Spartina patens*) and smooth cordgrass (*Spartina alterniflora*).

Salt haying took place in late August and early September. A 1908 article in the *Travel Magazine* titled "Early Autumn Days in Lyme" described a scene of salt haying: "Over Lyme broods the serene peace which is found only in a New England village....Here, all day the countrymen with long sweeping scythe mow down the salt hay and pitch it on great carts drawn by big brown oxen, gentle-eyed and slow. Or the hay is poled downstream in weatherbeaten scows by equally picturesque boatmen, strong and lithe."

While the salt haying process may have seemed romantic and evocative to writers and artists, it was, in fact, a lengthy, arduous task. According to *The Lieutenant River* by Susan Hollingsworth Ely and Elizabeth Plympton, "Farmers, accompanied by their sons and hired men, with oxen-drawn hay wagons, either backed up to a marsh, or more frequently went by scow to the meadows. The salt hay was cut by hand using a scythe.... The blade had to be sharpened after every hundred feet or so of hay was cut. Cut hay was usually piled into heaps....then two slim poles were slid

Salt Haying time at Lyme. *Old Lyme Historical Society Archive.*

underneath and two men—one at each end—picked up the load and carried it to a scow for transportation back to a landing, or if the ground was high, to a wagon."

Many farmers owned salt marsh land, and those who did not bought or bartered for the right to harvest the salt hay. The marshes were maintained through a system of ditching. The ditches were indicators of the often-informal boundaries and were also used as a way to drain low areas. The 1916 Connecticut State Agricultural Report corroborates this, saying, "Formerly the marshes of Lyme and Saybrook were regarded as of more value than at present as sources of salt hay and were ditched frequently so as to allow tidewater to drain off as this increases the hay yield and improves its quality. Some of the meadows are still ditched for this purpose but on many of them the ditches are no longer maintained."

Early disputes over mooring and harvesting rights led the towns to establish public town landings, which could be used by everyone to access the salt marshes. The right to harvest salt hay was seen as similar to the right to use the town green or common pasture. Many of the town landings that were designated for salt haying are still in use today as coastal access points and boat launches, but their very existence is testimony to the importance of salt haying rights and free coastal access to early settlers.

Oxen and draft horses were not only used for farming but also for many other kinds of heavy work, including logging, transportation of heavy loads and sometimes even moving a house or building from one location to another. This was accomplished by jacking up the building from its foundation and

Salt Haying off Ferry Road. *Old Lyme Historical Society Archive.*

James Riddle's team of horses moving the old town hall down Lyme Street, 1921. *Old Lyme Historical Society Archive.*

loading it onto skids or log rollers. Teams of oxen or draft horses were hitched up and driven to pull the building to its new location. Katharine Ludington wrote of her family's old house (which had been the Parsons Tavern and later Phoebe Griffin Noyes' home and school) being moved down the street in 1893 by a team of oxen, "It was a sad day when the pilgrimage of the old house began and it went tottering and bumping across the green and down the road to the present site, escorted by the watchful skill of the Piersons, father and sons who were famous as movers and stone masons."

Many structures were moved in this fashion, even well into the twentieth century. In 1921, after the new Memorial Town Hall was built, the old town hall was moved by teams of oxen and draft horses to its new location farther down Lyme Street, where it became the Masonic Lodge (now a private home).

Oxen and draft horses were valuable commodities, and by the 1890s, grange fairs became the place to show and sell livestock in many rural communities. Lyme Grange no. 147 was organized in 1896, and the first Hamburg Fair was held in 1897. As Bruce Stark states in *History of the Hamburg Fair*, "The history of the Lyme Grange Fair illustrated many of the changes that have taken place in the town of Lyme in the twentieth century.

Since the Grange was organized for the purpose of promoting agriculture, it is not surprising that the founders passed a resolution in the Spring of 1897 to hold a fair "to show that we practice agriculture as well as preach it." Six months later the first fair was held. Advertisements promised "One hundred pair of Working Oxen & Matched Steers plus milch cows, young cattle and a 'Drawing Match.'"

The fair was a success, and the grangers were determined to expand their offerings the following year. To accomplish this, they purchased a building and property to be used as a fairground. Starting in 1898, the fair took on a form still recognizable to twenty-first century Hamburg Fair attendees: "displays of fruits and vegetables, fancy work...collections, and a band concert in the evening."

Then, as now, a main attraction was the livestock drawing contests, now called "ox pulls" and "horse pulls" or "pony pulls." Other parts of the country may thrill to truck and tractor pulls at the county fair, belching diesel and dragging weights with heavy machinery, but in Lyme, old traditions die hard—if ever—and few things are more anticipated than the annual ox pull at the Hamburg Fair. The smoke and roar of a motor is no competition for the snort and stamp of a team of oxen, exhorted by the driver, pulling five tons or more of stone behind them in the dust. If an ox doesn't want to

Oxen at the Hamburg Fair, 2019. *Michaelle Pearson.*

move or cooperate with his yoked partner, he will stand immobile as a glacial erratic. But a well-trained team of driver and oxen working together can clear the land, plow a field, carry a load or help build a town.

At the fair, people still gather on the bleachers, shaded from the relentless August sun by ancient trees, to witness the awesome power of draft oxen and horses. It is easy to imagine bygone days, when "one entry could consist of several yoke of livestock" and "yokes of five or eight pair of large, sleek oxen from one farm were not uncommon." Stark says the 1898 fair featured 215 yokes of oxen, plus thoroughbred Devon and Jersey cows, as well as "many cattle from Old Lyme which were exhibited but not entered into competition."

But twentieth-century industrial farming methods made it difficult for small, local farms to compete. Farmers began using tractors and trucks, greatly reducing the role of oxen and plow horses. Long strings of oxen were no longer seen walking up the hill en route to the fair. Stark says, "In 1916, 135 yoke, mostly Devons, were on the grounds and thereafter the number of pairs of oxen was only rarely reported. Thirty-seven yoke appeared on the grounds in 1929 and the next year the number had dropped to 32."

He also cites an article in the *Deep River New Era*, which stated, "At the 1919 fair, 'although the usual show of trained cattle was held' efforts to sell several yoke of oxen at auction proved unsuccessful."

By 1974, there were only a handful of working farms left in the Lymes, such as Tiffany Farms (Lyme), Scott's Orchards (East Lyme) and Hefflon Farm (Old Lyme), but it seemed that even these few stalwarts were numbered as curiosities and "relics of a bygone age." The *Gazette* called Hefflon Farm "the last farm in Old Lyme which still grows produce on its premises." Arthur and Margaret Hefflon grew fruits and vegetables on about thirty-eight acres near Black Hall from 1940 until 1981. In 1989, the land was sold, and the Old Lyme Planning Commission approved a twenty-six-lot subdivision plan for the neighborhood now known as Hefflon Farms.

Fortunately, residents of the Lymes were not eager to jump on the subdivision bandwagon. Plans were made to set aside open space for hiking, trails and land preservation. Towns began setting aside money for land acquisition in their annual budgets. Today, the Old Lyme Land Trust owns more than 1,000 acres of conservation land and manages conservation easements and partnerships with the Nature Conservancy and other groups. The town of Old Lyme has set aside $75,000 per year since 1998 for its open space fund. Lyme also sets aside money in its annual budget for open space, and the Lyme Land Conservation Trust manages more than one hundred properties and conservation easements and maintains more than thirty-five miles of trails. The East Lyme Land Trust owns more than 850 acres and manages conservation easements for another 42 acres.

Alongside the land trust movement, there was also growing interest from citizens of the Lymes to support local agriculture. In contrast to the national decline in the numbers of small farms, Connecticut began to slowly experience an increase in the number of small farms beginning in the 1990s. According to the 2012 U.S. Department of Agriculture census of agriculture:

Bucking the national trend, Connecticut farming has been growing for the past two decades. We now have nearly 6,000 farms, which may not seem like a lot, but it's a staggering 60 percent increase from the 3,754 farms we had in our state in 1982. At the same time, [Connecticut] farmland acreage remained relatively stable, which means that the size of an average farm has been trending down. As of 2012, an average Connecticut farm is 73 acres....More than 900 Connecticut farms harvested vegetables for sale in 2012, with bell peppers being the most popular crop. 880 Connecticut nurseries, greenhouses, floriculture and sod farms grew and sold almost $253 million worth of crops. 774 farms in Connecticut are raising cattle and calves....In 2012, our farms sold nearly $70 million worth of milk from cows. Connecticut's coastal area has hosted shellfish farms since

Colonial times. In 2012, our aquaculture industry sold nearly $20 million worth of seafood, primarily shellfish from Long Island Sound.

Many of these new farmers are young, college-educated and interested in sustainable and/or organic methods of farming. White Gate Farm in East Lyme was started in 1999 by Pauline Lord and David Harlow on a historic dairy farm that had not been active since the 1950s. They received their organic certification in 2000 and host "Dinners at the Farm" and cooking classes in addition to selling produce, eggs, poultry and flowers at the farm stand.

Baylee Drown was raised on a dairy farm in Michigan, and now she and Ryan Quinn are the owners of Long Table Farm, formerly known as Upper Pond Farm in Old Lyme and New Mercies Farm in Lyme—organic farms that embrace sustainable practices, and use "human power" as much as possible.

Having worked with oxen at Green Mountain College, she considered how to accomplish the difficult work of initial tilling without using heavy farm machinery. Baylee asked some friends with draft horses to help them plow their fields during their first five years of farming and hosted a demonstration with oxen, saying, "People still use oxen on small organic vegetable farms. It's coming back a little bit. Horses are generally faster than oxen and have a longer working life, but oxen are more utilitarian and less expensive to keep, and can thrive on lower quality forage, such as salt marsh hay."

Like Baylee and Quinn, many small organic farms start out with a Community Supported Agriculture (CSA) model. CSAs operate in the same way as futures shares. The farm sells shares of the upcoming season's harvest for a set price well before the planting season begins. The farmers use the CSA money to purchase seeds and other supplies. When the crops are harvested, the CSA members are given a share of the bounty. Depending on the size of the yield, the farm may also sell additional produce to restaurants or shops and vend at farmers markets.

The iconic Lyme Farmers Market started at Ashlawn Farm around 2001 and moved to Tiffany Farm in 2019. East Lyme has also held farmers markets for many years, including the thriving Niantic market, which started in 2009. Farm-to-table dinners and events have become very popular, as have restaurants that serve local produce, meat, seafood and poultry. Farm stands abound in Old Lyme, Lyme and East Lyme, offering fresh, local options for those wishing to seek them out. Local agriculture is clearly on the rise. People in Lyme, Old Lyme and East Lyme have embraced the rich history and tradition of farming here, from the still agriculturally focused Hamburg Fair to broad popular support for local farms and open space.

BEARING WITNESS—
THE BARBIZON OAK

It's hard to know exactly when it took root, but it was probably an acorn sprouting in the warm spring sun sometime between the passing of John Winthrop Jr. and the birth of Benjamin Franklin. By the time young George Washington was contemplating cherry trees, it was already a strong sapling shooting skyward. It was large enough to cast considerable shade by the time of the French and Indian War, and the soldiers of the American Revolution could have put down their packs to rest against it for a moment. When the Marquis de Lafayette was escorted by Moses Warren along the nearby Lyme–New London Turnpike, it was probably the highest landmark on the landscape. When the last of the Nehantics were living on their Black Point reservation, it had grown to a mighty tree. At the turn of the twentieth century, it caught the eye of famous Lyme painters, like tonalist Henry Ward Ranger, who immortalized it in oil on canvas. Childe Hassam ridiculed Ranger's work as being of the "Baked Apple School," but the autumnal browns and oranges of Ranger's 1902 painting *Autumn Woodlands* perfectly capture the spirit and nature of the Barbizon oak.

It is a white oak, over three hundred years old, with a circumference of sixteen and a half feet. With its massive branches reaching out, dropping autumn leaves large enough to cover a person's face, it's easy to see why the white oak is Connecticut's state tree. While it may not be the largest white oak in the country, how many other trees can boast of being the subject of a masterpiece by one of America's great painters? The community of painters in Lyme in 1900 came to be known as the American Barbizon,

The Barbizon oak. *Kate Brown.*

and the oak they so revered as a landmark came to be named after them. It stands today, easily accessible at the entrance of Old Lyme's open space at the end of Wyckford Road behind the Old Lyme Inn (once called the Barbizon Oak Inn).

While the roar of nearby I-95 can sometimes be heard over the songbird's tune and the raptor's call, and while bureaucrats draw preposterous lines on maps with their rulers, proposing high-speed rail lines by its roots, there is something about the Barbizon oak that partakes of the eternal. When the late summer zephyr blows through its canopy of leaves, it sounds the song of nature itself, and one can almost hear the voice of the Barbizon oak intoning the sacred hymn of this land. If we could only understand the words—oh, what a story it could tell us.

BIBLIOGRAPHY

Allyn, Adeline Bartlett. *Black Hall Traditions and Reminiscences*. Hartford, CT: Case, Lockwood and Brainerd Co., 1908.

Andrews, E. Benjamin. *History of the United States*. New York: Charles Scribner's Sons, 1895.

Bachman, Robert. *An Illustrated History of Waterford, CT*. Waterford, CT: Bicentennial Committee, 2000

Barker, G. Stuart. *Landmarks of Old Lyme: The Beginnings of the Town*. 3rd ed. Old Lyme, CT: Ladies' Library Association of Old Lyme, 1968.

Bourque, Edmund C., ed. *East Lyme Public Library 1897–1997: One Hundred Years of Growth*. Niantic, CT, East Lyme Public Library, 1998.

Burr, Jean Chandler. *Lyme Records 1667–1730*. Stonington, CT: Pequot Press, 1968.

Burt, Sarah Sill Welles. *Old Silltown: Something of Its History and People*. N.p., 1912.

Chapman, L.E., and E.H. Murphy. *Scallop Shells and Granite Too: East Lyme, Connecticut 1839–1989*. Mystic, CT: Mystic Publications, 1989.

Chendali, Olive Tubbs. *Stories of East Lyme*. Niantic, CT: East Lyme Public Library, 2001.

Chendali, Olive Tubbs, Jane Moore Fattori and Lyle Edgecomb Chapman. *East Lyme: Our Town and How It Grew*. Mystic, CT: Mystic Publications, 1989.

Dale, T. Nelson, and Herbert E. Gregory. *The Granites of Connecticut*. Washington, D.C.: U.S. Geological Survey, 1911.

DeForest, John W. *History of the Indians of Connecticut.* Hartford, CT: Wm. Jas. Hamersley, 1852.

Disla, Alex, and Alicia Cook. *How to Build the Brockway Skiff.* Rewritten by Timothy Visel for the Sound School Industry Workshop Series. Maritime Education Network, 2001.

Douglass, Frederick. *Narrative of the Life of Frederick Douglass, an American Slave.* London: G. Kershaw and Son, 1852.

Dwight, Theodore. *The History of Connecticut.* New York: Harper and Brothers, 1840.

East Lyme Historical Society. Little Boston School.

Ely, Caro Weir. *Lest We Forget.* Privately published, 1965.

Ernesty, Frederick O. *Highways, Holdings and Landmarks in the Ancient Town of Lyme.* Vol. 2, part 5 of *Records and Papers of the New London County Historical Society.* New London, CT: New London County Historical Society, 1904.

Federal Writers' Project. *Connecticut: A Guide to Its Roads, Lore and People.* Boston, MA: Houghton Mifflin, 1938.

———. *U.S. One, Maine to Florida.* New York: Modern Age Books, 1938.

Griswold, Wick. *Connecticut Pirates and Privateers.* Charleston, SC: The History Press, 2015.

———. *Griswold Point.* Charleston, SC: The History Press, 2014.

Hale, Charles R., and Mary H Babin. *Headstone Inscriptions: Town of East Lyme, Connecticut.* Hartford, CT: [s.n.], 1937.

Harding, James E. *Lyme Yesterdays: How Our Forefathers Made a Living on the Connecticut Shore.* Stonington, CT: Pequot Press, 1967.

Hodges, Graham Russell Gao. *David Ruggles.* Chapel Hill: University of North Carolina Press, 2010.

Jewett, Doris "Doad" Reynolds. *Things Remembered.* Deep River, CT: Valley Press and New Era Co., 2005.

Kuchta, E.H., E.H. Murphy, N.D. Kalal and L. Lange. *Factories, Farms and Fishes Too: Historical Photographs of East Lyme, Connecticut.* East Lyme, CT: East Lyme Historical Society, 2010.

Kuzmeskus, Elaine M. *Connecticut in the Golden Age of Spiritualism.* Charleston SC: The History Press, 2016.

Little, J. David. *Revolutionary Lyme: A Portrait, 1765–1783.* Old Lyme, CT: Board of Finance, Town of Old Lyme, 1976.

Ludington, Katharine. *Lyme and Our Family.* Privately printed, 1928.

Lundgren, Lawrence. *Bedrock Geology of the Hamburg Quadrangle.* Hartford, CT: State Geological and Natural History Survey of Connecticut, 1966.

McNatt, Kasey, and Lesley Crawford. *Legends of Our Towns: East Lyme and Salem*. East Lyme, CT: self-published, 1997.

Oliver, Sandra L. *Saltwater Foodways*. Mystic, CT: Mystic Seaport Museum, 1970.

Proceedings at the Opening of the Phoebe Griffin Noyes Library. Old Lyme, CT: privately printed, 1898.

Roberts, George S. *Historic Towns of the Connecticut River Valley*. Schenectady, NY: Robson & Adee, 1906.

Rogers, Sophie Selden. *Selden Ancestry: A Family History, Giving the Ancestors and Descendants of George Shattuck Selden and His Wife, Elizabeth Wright Clark*. Oil City, PA: Edwin van Deusen Seldon, 1931.

Schuler, Stanley, ed. *Hamburg Cove*. Old Lyme, CT: Lyme Historical Society, Florence Griswold Museum, n.d.

Simmons, William S. *Spirit of the New England Tribes*. Lebanon, NH: University Press of New England, 1986.

Slater, James A. *The Colonial Burying Grounds of Eastern Connecticut*. New Haven: Connecticut Academy of Arts and Sciences, 1996.

Smith, Jane T. *Last of the Nehantics*. East Lyme, CT: East Lyme Public Library, 2011.

Speck, Frank G. *Notes on the Mohegan and Niantic Indians*. Vol. 3 of *Anthropological Papers of the Museum of Natural History*. New York: Order of the Trustees, 1909.

———. *Remnants of the Nehantics*. N.p.: Southern Workman, 1918.

Stark, Bruce P. *Promoting the Interests of Agriculture: A History of the Hamburg Fair 1897–1941*. Lyme, CT: Lyme Grange, 2001.

Strother, Horatio T. *The Underground Railroad in Connecticut*. Middletown, CT: Wesleyan University Press, 1962.

Tantaquidgeon, Gladys. *Folk Medicine of the Delaware and Related Algonkian Indians*. Harrisburg: Pennsylvania Historical and Museum Commission, 2001.

Tatum, Alma Merry. *For the Love of Books*. Old Lyme, CT: Friends of the Old Lyme–Phoebe Griffin Noyes Library, 1997.

Trowbridge, Bertha Chadwick, and Charles McLean Andrews. *Old Houses of Connecticut*. New Haven, CT: Yale University Press, 1923.

Withington, Sydney. *The First Twenty Years of Railroads in Connecticut*. No. 45 of *Tercentenary Commission of the State of Connecticut*. New Haven, CT: Yale University Press, 1935. Microfilm.

Wordell, David H. *The Quarries of Selden Neck*. 1980. Videodisc, 46 min.

Interviews

Abigail Stokes, Pine Grove historian. Interview with author, 2019.
Baylee Drown, Long Table Farm. Interview with author, 2019
Mark Lander, Old Lyme Historical Society. Email interview with author.
2019

Archives

David Peters Railroad Collection. Thomas. J. Dodd Research Center. University of Connecticut Library.
Blood Street Sculls/Old Lyme Rowing Association Papers. Old Lyme Historical Society Archives
Joseph A. Caples Papers. Lyme Public Hall and Local History Archives.
Leroy Roberts Railroad Collection. Thomas. J. Dodd Research Center. University of Connecticut Library.
McCurdy-Salisbury Family Papers. Old Lyme Historical Society Archive.
Nehantic Tribe Papers. Indian and Colonial Research Center, Old Mystic, CT.
Pfeiffer, John. *Duck River Cemetery 1676–1735*. Old Lyme Historical Society Archives.
———. *Slavery in Southeastern Connecticut: A View from Lyme*. Old Lyme Historical Society Archives.
Elizabeth Huey Putnam Papers. Lyme Public Hall and Local History Archives.
Records of Andrew Griswold, J.P. Lyme, CT 1784–1810. Connecticut State Library.
Then and Now: Lending Libraries of Lyme. Lyme Public Hall, 2013.
Warren, Moses. Journal. East Lyme Historical Society Archive.

Newspapers

Banner of Light (Spiritualist Press)
Connecticut Eastern News
Connecticut Gazette
Connecticut Journal
Deep River New Era

East Lyme Star
Gazette (shoreline)
Hartford Courant
New London Daily Star
New London Day
Newport Mercury
Newport News
New York Times
Niantic Herald
Sound Breeze

Periodicals

Bulletin of the Connecticut Historical Society. April 1949.

Freedom's Journal. April 4, 1828.

Gencarella, Stephen Olbrys. "The Selden Cove Lotus" *Connecticut Explored* (Spring 2019).

Green, Samuel. *Green's Almanac and Register for the State of Connecticut*. New London, 1797.

New Haven and New London Railroad Annual Report 1854. New Haven and New London, CT, 1854.

New York, New Haven, and Hartford Railroad, Co. Annual Report 1890. New York: William H. Clark, 1890.

Pfeiffer, John. "Post-Contact Populations of the Nehantic Reservation of Lyme, CT." *Bulletin of the Archaeological Society of Connecticut* 59 (1996).

Rags in Paper, No. 4., 1928. Rag Content Paper Manufacturers, Box 245, Springfield, MA.

Sisson, William. "Fish Cutter." *Anglers Journal*, August 12, 2016.

Jim Lampos and Michaelle Pearson. *Chris Devlin, Devlin Photography.*

About the Authors

JIM LAMPOS received his bachelor of arts degree in sociology (summa cum laude) from Brandeis University, where he was inducted into Phi Beta Kappa. He completed the General Course at the London School of Economics and was awarded a Kaplan Fellowship to attend the New School for Social Research, where he received his master of arts in urban affairs and policy analysis. Jim is a published poet and musician, who has released eight CDs, toured nationally and been featured on network television.

MICHAELLE PEARSON holds a bachelor of arts in journalism from Creighton University and a juris doctor degree from New York Law School. She was director of copy at Arnell Group and continues to work as a freelance writer and editor. Michaelle is a member of the Old Lyme–Phoebe Griffin Noyes Library board, the New York Genealogical and Biological Society, the Connecticut Society of Genealogists and is cochair of the Old Lyme Historical Society.

The husband-and-wife team of Lampos and Pearson have also written *Revolution in the Lymes: From the New Lights to the Sons of Liberty* (The History Press, 2016), *Remarkable Women of Old Lyme* (The History Press, 2015) and *Rum Runners, Governors, Beachcombers and Socialists* (Old Lyme Historical Society, 2010).

Visit us at
www.historypress.com
....